أهلاً وسهلاً

الحروف العربية وأصواتها

أهلاً وسهلاً

العربية الوظيفية للمبتدئين
الطبعة الثانية

حروف العربية وأصواتها

مهدي العش

منقحة مع آلن كلارك

دار جامعة ييل للنشر
نيو هيفن ولندن

Ahlan wa Sahlan

Functional Modern Standard Arabic for Beginners
Second Edition

Letters and Sounds of the Arabic Language
With Online Media

Mahdi Alosh

Revised with Allen Clark

Yale UNIVERSITY PRESS
New Haven and London

This book was originally accompanied by an
audio CD and a DVD. The audio and video
files are now available at
yalebooks.com/ahlan.
To access them, use the password aleppo.

Publisher: Mary Jane Peluso
Editorial Assistant: Elise Panza
Project Editor: Timothy Shea
Manuscript Editor: Karen Hohner
Production Editor: Ann-Marie Imbornoni
Production Controller: Karen Stickler
Designer: Mary Valencia
Typesetter: J. P. Kang

Printed in the United States of America.

ISBN: 978-0-300-21446-8

10 9 8 7 6 5 4 3 2

محتويات الكتاب

Contents

Introduction

Letters and Sounds of the Arabic Language has been designed as a workbook to accompany *Ahlan wa Sahlan,* Second Edition, but it may also be used independently as an introduction to Arabic orthography, basic words and phrases, and culture.

This workbook is divided into six units; most units begin with a presentation of some basic language functions (e.g., greeting people, introducing oneself, describing one's place of origin) accompanied by comprehension activities based on the audio program and the DVD. Cultural notes describe some of the conventions related to these conversational exchanges; the workbook also contains an introduction to the Arab states and political systems, as well as a discussion of some regional differences in Arabic.

The introduction of these basic conversational exchanges achieves a threefold objective: establishing a communicative classroom, honing learner listening and speaking skills, and whetting the student's desire to hold authentic conversations outside of class. DVD scenes support all of the workbook's communicative activities and offer a window into how the phrases are used in context. After viewing the DVD scenes, students are provided with communicative exercises that not only help them learn the phrases, but also foster a sense of community by promoting authentic interaction with their classroom peers.

The Arabic script is introduced letter by letter, with groupings dependent on the shape of the shell. Each letter progresses through a six-phase introduction: (1) providing a chart that illustrates the letter's four positions (initial, medial, final, and independent); (2) presenting a diagram of how the letter is drawn, using shaded arrows for guidance; (3) tracing the letter in all of its positions in words accompanied by illustrations; (4) practicing the letter in all of its positions; (5) tracing full words; and then (6) writing those words. Listening exercises such as word recognition and dictation reinforce the relationship between the letters introduced in that unit and their associated sounds. Units conclude with recognition exercises in which the letters are used within an authentic context such as maps, newspaper clippings, or advertisements.

We include four appendixes at the back of the workbook for easy reference: Appendix A contains the Arabic alphabet with the different forms of the letters according to their positions in the word and the Roman symbol representing each letter. Appendix B contains a key to the sound system of Arabic and the transliteration system used in this workbook (that is, the Roman symbols used to represent Arabic letters). Appendix C contains an answer key to all of the discrete-answer exercises in the workbook, including listening and DVD exercises. Appendix D contains the DVD scripts.

At the end of the book, there is a cumulative glossary, or dictionary, containing all the words found in the vocabulary lists at the end of the units, as well as key words from the listening and DVD passages. The vocabulary in the cumulative glossary is marked with the lesson number where each word first appears. Although in the initial stage (see the vocabulary list at the end of each unit) we use transliteration in order to facilitate the learning process for the beginner, we use it sparingly, to exemplify sounds or letters that students have not learned yet; in the cumulative vocabulary transliteration is not used.

Letters and Sounds of the Arabic Language is merely one component of the Ahlan wa Sahlan educational package, which presents the learner with multiple avenues to explore Arabic: this workbook, the textbook, the video program, the audio program, and an online interactive exercise program.

To access the audio, video, and
Online Interactive Exercise Program, go to
yalebooks.com/ahlan
Password: **aleppo**

We provide the instructor with an Annotated Instructor's Edition of the textbook and online resources that include lesson plans, handouts, exercises, texts, and examinations to facilitate the use of the textbook and its supplementary materials.

To the Student

What is the key to learning a foreign language well? Before you embark on your journey in learning Arabic using this instructional package, you may wish to take some time to reflect on this question. Over the past decade, students have offered nearly every conceivable answer after I pose it on the first day of my Arabic classes. The answer that I have become convinced is "correct" is: *to think in the language.* No matter what your original answer may have been, thinking in the language is central to learning a language well by practicing it on a minute-by-minute basis. This is possible even at the very beginning of your Arabic studies by containing your thoughts in Arabic, using an internal banter as practice, and gradually widening the scope of language use by introducing new words into your repertoire. Make this language your own by actively seeking out those vocabulary words that you use in your mother tongue. These are the words with which you will be expressing yourself and that, in turn, will create an Arabic persona. The more you practice, the more permanent your learning becomes and the stronger your individuality will become in Arabic. We encourage you to actively surround yourself with the language as much as possible, and we have made this quite easy for you in fact. Simply by visiting our Web site at **www.yalebooks.com/ ahlan**, you can download all of *Letters and Sounds of the Arabic Language*'s video and audio materials so that you may listen to or watch them wherever you are and whenever you wish.

Much has been said about the difficulty of learning Arabic. In fact, the United States government lists Arabic as a Category 4 language—among the most difficult for an American to learn. You may view the notion of difficulty in one of two ways: as an obstacle or as a challenge. We tend to think that Arabic is not so much difficult for the Western learner as it is different. According to studies completed in 2006 in which Arabic grammar was compared to other world languages, it was found that verb conjugation in Arabic is logical (less complex than Spanish), its tense system is easier than English, and given that Arabic is a root-derivational language, it is quite mathematical and elegant in its dexterity—meaning that it is able to accommodate new concepts using its derivational qualities. What this means for you is that you can not only learn Arabic, but learn it well.

We designed *Ahlan wa Sahlan* and the *Letters and Sounds of the Arabic Language* workbook to guide you on the most direct learning path to achieve functional language goals and proficiency. It is our hope that this workbook will serve not only to anticipate pitfalls, but also to allow you to experience the joy of learning one of the oldest living languages on the planet and the riches that it has to offer.

To the Instructor

Letters and Sounds of the Arabic Language introduces learners of Arabic to the language's sound and writing systems and provides them with basic structural and lexical knowledge that will enable them to communicate in Arabic and maintain interest in the study of the language. In the Second Edition of *Ahlan wa Sahlan,* the workbook was separated from the textbook in order to make learning the Arabic sounds and letters more manageable and to focus more on the mechanics of reading and writing in addition to introducing language functions.

Letters and Sounds of the Arabic Language, used in conjunction with *Ahlan wa Sahlan,* Second Edition, and the accompanying supplementary material, attempts to provide a learning environment conducive to effective acquisition of specific language abilities. These abilities, in their totality, create a measure of proficiency in Arabic. Upon completing this course, the average learner may achieve a proficiency level within the Intermediate Mid range established by the American Council on the Teaching of Foreign Languages (ACTFL). Naturally, results vary with respect to individual learner differences and may range between higher or lower proficiency levels.

Mahdi Alosh
Professor of Arabic and Applied Linguistics
Mahdi.Alosh@gmail.com

Allen Clark
Instructional Assistant Professor
The University of Mississippi
University, MS 38677

Acknowledgments

I am indebted to so many individuals whose contributions improved the quality of this work, including students of Arabic at various institutions inside and outside the United States as well as colleagues who used the first edition and took time out of their busy schedules to provide me with feedback. I am especially indebted to my wife, Ibtissam, for putting up with the endless hours I spent on developing the material and for designing and programming the computer-assisted program that accompanied the first edition. I would like to acknowledge the extraordinary assistance and input by Allen Clark, who serves as a co-author of the second edition. He brings with him extensive experience in teaching the first edition as well as the perspective of the learner and the specialist. I also appreciate the expert assistance of Fayez Al-Ghalayini, whose meticulous editing of the Arabic portion of this textbook and assiduous input and profuse comments on the grammatical aspect improved the quality of this work and made it more accurate. I thank Lalainya Goldsberry, Hiba Abdallah, and Nevine Demian for providing factual and cultural information about Egypt. The peripheral materials associated with the textbook have received much assistance from several individuals. The online program has gone through several phases to which Abdulkafi Albirini, Allen Clark, Hanan Kashou, Rick Trinkle, Farah Combs, and J. C. Raymond contributed, each one in his or her area of expertise. I am also indebted to Khaled Huthaily, whose meticulous work on the program has made it more user friendly and effective. I thank Nonie Williams and Lana Khodary for the many hours they devoted to the recording of the audio material. I recognize the quality work by Dima Barakat and Maya Pastalides in designing, scripting, shooting, and producing the video program.

Finally, I thank the outside reviewers, whose comments on the manuscript and suggestions for improvements are gratefully appreciated:

Shukri Abed, Middle East Institute
Carl Sharif El-Tobgui, Brandeis University
Ghazi Abu-Hakema, Middlebury College
Abdulkafi Albirini, University of Illinois, Urbana-Champaign
Roger Allen, University of Pennsylvania
Muhammad Aziz, Yale University
Elizabeth Bergman, Georgetown University
Mirena Christoff, Brown University
Liljana Elverskog, University of North Texas
Fadia Hamid, Chagrin Falls Schools, Ohio
Eric Lewis
Summer Loomis, University of Washington, Seattle
Oraib Mango, Arizona State University
Ellen McLarney, Stanford University
David J. Mehall, University of Maryland
Harry Neale, University of California, Berkeley
Waheed Samy, University of Michigan

الوَحدةُ الأولى

Unit One

Objectives

- Learning two common greetings
- Introducing oneself
- Taking leave
- Introduction to the one-way connectors اودذرز
- Introduction to the Arabic numbers ١–١٠

---

1. Common Greetings

There are several common greetings used in Arabic, and here we have chosen to introduce two of the most frequent. The greeting represented above is roughly equivalent to the English greeting-response "hi–hello." The first woman says *marḥaban* and the second woman responds *ahlan*. As in English, the response may repeat the greeting ("hi–hi" or in Arabic *marḥaban–marḥaban*) or use a different word ("hi–hello" or in Arabic *marḥaban–ahlan*), as is the case here.

■ **Cultural Note:** This greeting can be said to anyone at any time of the day.

The greeting above is one of the most common in the Arab and Islamic worlds. Literally *as-salāmu 'alaykum* means "peace be upon you," but functions as "hello." It can be addressed to a single person or a group of people in any situation, formal or informal. The response to this greeting is *wa 'alaykumu s-salām* meaning "and upon you peace."

■ **Cultural Note:** One of this greeting's functions is to announce one's presence when entering a home or a room. It is the obligation of one or more of the people present to respond audibly. Further, you may use it even if its use would interrupt some activity that is going on, such as a conversation. Many people, when greeting or upon responding to a greeting, place the right hand on the chest, as the man on the left is doing. You will notice that the response has the reverse word order of the greeting.

2. Introducing Oneself 🔊

١- أنا ياسِر.

٤- تَشَرَّفْنا.

٢- تَشَرَّفْنا.

٣- أنا رَنا.

When meeting someone for the first time, you may introduce yourself by saying *anā* أنا ("I am . . .") plus your name, or you can say *ismī* اِسْمي ("my name is . . .") plus your name. The other person responds by saying *tašarrafnā* تَشَرَّفْنا, which is roughly equivalent to "pleased to meet you" (literally: "we've been honored"). The exchange is repeated with the other person saying his or her name.

3. Leave-Taking 🔊

مَعَ السَلامَة.

إلى اللِقاء.

Just like other greetings, leave-taking involves two different phrases. The phrase *ilā lliqā'* إلى اللِقاء is roughly equivalent to "I'll see you later." The response phrase *ma'a s-salāma* مَعَ السَلامَة literally means "[go] with safety." Normally, the phrase *ma'a s-salāma* مَعَ السَلامَة is said by the person(s) staying behind, but it can also be used by the one leaving, as is the case in many regions, including the Gulf.

Exercise ١ ❖ ١ تمرين

Watch DVD Unit 1: When you are watching the DVD, become an active participant by repeating what you hear, trying to imitate the sounds and inflections used in the scenes.

Dialogue 1: Circle the best choice:

1. What are the names of the two speakers?

a.	Name of Speaker 1	b.	Name of Speaker 2
	Samir		Nadim
	Adnan		Sharif
	Saeed		Nabil
	Ayman		Shukry

2. How did Speaker 1 say "pleased to meet you"?
   a. *tašarrafnā*
   b. *furṣa saʿīda*
   c. *ismī sāmir*

Dialogue 2: Circle the best choice:

1. What are the names of the two speakers?

a.	Name of the young woman	b.	Name of the young man
	Muna		Nadim
	Kristine		Abd Allah
	Hala		Ahmad
	Manal		Salim

2. How did the young woman say "hello" to the young man?
   a. *wa anā ayḍan*
   b. *as-salāmu ʿalaykum*
   c. *maʿa s-salāma*
   d. *furṣa saʿīda*

Unit 1   4

Conversation: Try to hold your first conversation in Arabic with a classmate. To complete this task you must remember (1) to greet your classmate; (2) to introduce yourself; and (3) to say good-bye. Try to use both of the introductions that you learned in this lesson. Endeavor to meet as many of your classmates as you can. Notice that the more you practice, the more fluent you become.

- This is a culturally authentic conversation, so why not try it out with some speakers of Arabic that you know outside the class? *Practice not only makes perfect, it makes permanent.*

4. The Arabic Alphabet: One-Way Connectors

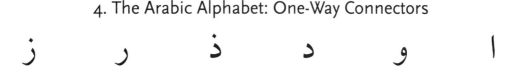

The Arabic phonetic system is easy to learn and master because the Arabic alphabet has a high correspondence between sound and symbol. This means that a letter is pronounced almost the same regardless of its position in a word.

The Arabic alphabet contains twenty-eight letters in addition to the *hamza* and two variants of existing letters (see the alphabet chart in Appendix A). A number of diacritical marks complement the alphabet. Diacritical marks are signs written above or below the letters. Words are written and read from right to left.

Arabic is written cursively in that the letters connect to one another. However, some letters only connect to preceding letters, or from the right side. These are known as one-way connectors. The table on the following page lists them along with their pronunciations.

One-Way Connectors			
Sound Example	Symbol	Name	Letter
dad, far	*ā*	*alif* أَلِف	ا
boot, wet	*ū, w*	*wāw* واو	و
dim	*d*	*dāl* دال	د
then	*ḏ*	*ḏāl* ذال	ذ
trilled **r**	*r*	*rā'* راء	ر
busy	*z*	*zāy* زاي	ز

Examine how each of the letters below is written, proceeding from right to left. Strokes are made from right to left and from top to bottom. If there is a dot, it is placed after the letter is drawn. Note that the letters *wāw* (و), *rā'* (ر), and *zāy* (ز) are curved and descend slightly below the line, whereas *dāl* (د) and *ḏāl* (ذ) are angled and do not descend below the line.

A. The Letter *alif* (ا)

This letter is written from top to bottom in the independent position, but if it is connected to a preceding letter, it is drawn from bottom up. Remember that the *alif* never connects to a letter following it. In other words, the letter following the *alif* will always be in the initial position. The long vowel *ā* represented by this letter has two variations, as in the vowels in English "far" and "dad."

Drawing an *alif*:

Connected from the right	Independent
ﻟ	ﺍ

تمرين ٣ ❖ Exercise 3

Trace over the gray letters: The *alif* appears in its independent and connected forms.

كِتاب   غَزال

تمرين ٤ ❖ Exercise 4

Tracing: Trace over the gray letters and copy them several times on a ruled sheet of paper. Remember to write from right to left.

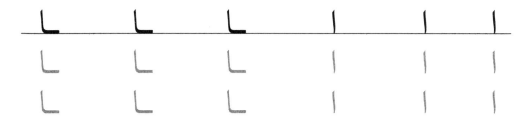

B. The Letter *wāw* (و)

The letter *wāw* (و) functions as both a vowel (as in "b<u>oo</u>t") and a semivowel which has a consonantal value (as in "<u>w</u>et"). It is easy to distinguish between the two because an Arabic syllable does not start with a vowel, nor does it allow two vowels consecutively. Thus, any و followed or preceded by a vowel is certainly a semivowel. Consider the following examples of *wāw*:

1. واد   consonant (followed by a vowel)

2. دود   vowel (preceded and followed by consonants)

3. داوود   consonant (preceded and followed by vowels)

Example 1 is made up of a consonant و and a vowel ا (CV); example 2 contains a consonant د, a vowel و, and another consonant د (CVC); while example 3 contains two syllables, دا and وود. When the two syllables of example 3 are joined, they produce the typical Arabic word structure (CVCVC), where consonants and vowels alternate. Two general rules follow:

- ■ **Rule 1**: An Arabic syllable always starts with a consonant, never with a vowel.
- ■ **Rule 2**: Two vowels do not occur consecutively in a syllable.

Drawing a *wāw*:

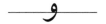

Finish under the line	Go around	Start on the line

Trace over the gray letters:

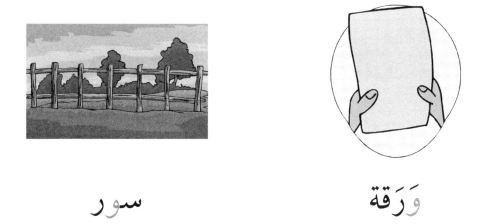

ورَقة   سور

C. The Letter *rā'* (ر)

The Arabic *r* sound is very different from the American *r*. The Arabic *r* resembles the *r* sound in the Spanish word *pero*, where the tip of the tongue flaps against the alveolar ridge behind the upper front teeth (see **The Organs of Speech** in Unit 3). The Arabic *r* sounds more or less like the *t* sound in "auto" and "writer." By contrast, the American *r* is vowel-like.

Drawing the ر or ز:

Connected from the right	Independent
ـرّ	ر

Place your pencil above the line starting at the top of the letter and draw a curved line downwards and slightly to the left in one stroke. The bottom of the ر and the ز go beneath the line. The ز is written in precisely the same manner as the ر, with the exception of the dot placed directly over it. Remember that the dots in Arabic are written after the word has been finished, just like dotting an "i" in English when writing in cursive.

ر

_____

ز

_____

Trace over the gray letters: These letters appear in their independent and connected forms.

سَرير

ثَوْر

جَزَر

مَوْز

D. The Letters *dāl* (د) and *ḏāl* (ذ)

Connected from the right	Independent
لد	د

Place your pencil above the line starting at the top of the letter and draw a roughly 45 degree angle to create both the *dāl* and the *ḏāl*. The only difference between the two letters is the dot above the *ḏāl*.

_____ د

_____ ذ

Trace over the gray letters: These letters appear in their independent and connected forms.

بَدو

دَجاج

مُذيع

ذُرَة

تمرين ٨ ❖ Exercise 8

Trace over the gray letters: Remember to write from right to left. Your strokes should go from top to bottom.

ز	ر	ذ	د	و	ا
ز	ر	ذ	د	و	ا
ز	ر	ذ	د	و	ا

Drawing letters: See how many times you can write the same letter on each line.

ا

و

د

ذ

ر

ز

E. Combining Sounds/Letters into Syllables and Words

The combination of د and ا is pronounced *dā*: د + ا = دا. Add another د to the end of the syllable and you get a word: داد. Try to sound it out.

Likewise, the letters ز and ا make the syllable زا. What is the syllable made by combining the letters ر and و؟ Write it down in this blank _____, moving from right to left. Now combine the first and second syllables into one word and write it down in this blank _____.

F. Distinguishing among Similar Letters

The letter *ḏāl* ذ (*ḏ*) differs from *dāl* د (*d*) only by a dot placed above it (ذ). The letter *rā'* ر (*r*) differs from *dāl* د in the way it is drawn. Instead of the angled shape of د, it has a slanting, curved shape and it descends slightly below the line (ر). The letter *zāy* ز (*z*) is written like ر but with a dot above it. Therefore, it is important to attend to the placement and number of dots of particular letters.

- Keep in mind that one-way connectors do not connect to each other.

Exercise 10 ❖ ١٠ تمرین

Listen and write: Listen to each word and repeat during the pause, then trace over the gray words. Pronounce each word as you copy it. Note that the letters ر ز و descend slightly below the line, whereas د ذ and ا do not.

زود   ذاد   زار   واز   راد   دود

Exercise 11 ❖ ١١ تمرین

Forming words: See how many times you can write the same word on each line.

دود _____

راد _____

واز _____

زار _____

ذاد _____

زود _____

Exercise 12 ❖ ١٢ تمرین

Listen and repeat: Listen to each word and repeat during the pause. Remember to read from right to left. There are two items on each line:

زور	2-	زاد	1-
دارو	4-	ذود	3-
دوراد	6-	زادو	5-
زاد	8-	داوود	7-
رادود	10-	واد	9-
وازو	12-	زورو	11-

تمرین ۱۳ ❖ Exercise 13

Listen and recognize: Listen as one word from each pair is read to you and check the box next to the appropriate word. Remember to read from right to left.

☐ رادو	☐ دارو	۱-
☐ راز	☐ زار	۲-
☐ راوا	☐ وار	۳-
☐ ذاد	☐ زاد	۴-
☐ رود	☐ زود	۵-
☐ زارو	☐ رازو	۶-
☐ داوو	☐ وادو	۷-
☐ داذ	☐ ذاد	۸-

تمرین ۱٤ ❖ Exercise 14

Spelling: Join the letters in each set to form words, as in the example. Then indicate whether the letter *wāw* (و) represents a consonant or a vowel and explain why. Note that one-way connectors do not connect to each other. Refer to section 4B for an explanation of when the *wāw* acts as a consonant or a vowel.

Vowel	Consonant		
☑	☐	داذود ــــــــ	مِثال : د + ا + ذ + و + د =

Explanation: *Preceded and followed by consonants*

Vowel	Consonant		
☐	☐	ــــــــ	= ز + ا + ر + ر + و -۱
☐	☐	ــــــــ	= د + و + ذ + ا -۲
☐	☐	ــــــــ	= ر + ا + و + ا + د -۳
☐	☐	ــــــــ	= و + ا + د + ا + د -٤
☐	☐	ــــــــ	= ز + ا + د + و + ر -۵

Dictation: Listen to the words and syllables dictated to you and write them down in the blank spaces next to item numbers.

_____ –2	_____ –1
_____ –4	_____ –3
_____ –6	_____ –5
_____ –8	_____ –7
_____ –10	_____ –9

5. A Quick Look at Numbers

Until the Arabic numerals are covered, the following numeral conversion chart will help you recognize the numbers in exercise items.

Numeral Conversion Chart									
0	1	2	3	4	5	6	7	8	9
٠	١	٢	٣	٤	٥	٦	٧	٨	٩

Spelling: Add the letters together to make a word, and then spell the word out phonetically in the second blank space. For phonetic spelling, consult the table titled **One-Way Connectors** on page 6. Follow the example:

dāwūd _____	داوود _____	مِثال : د + ا + و + و + د =
_____	_____	١- د + ا + ز =
_____	_____	٢- د + ا + د =
_____	_____	٣- د + ا + ر =
_____	_____	٤- د + ا + و =
_____	_____	٥- ذ + ا + ذ + ا + ر =
_____	_____	٦- و + ا + و =
_____	_____	٧- د + و + د =
_____	_____	٨- ر + ا + ز + ا + و =
_____	_____	٩- ز + ا + د + و + ذ =
_____	_____	١٠- ر + و + ا + ذ =

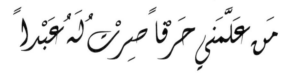

"I am eternally indebted to whoever teaches me as much as a single letter."

Recognition: Examine these excerpts from the Arabic print media and identify the letters ا و د ذ ر ز by circling them. Check the answer key to confirm your answers.

درجات الحرارة العظمى والصغرى المتوقعة
اليوم ١٨/٣٢. زخات من المطر بعد الظهر.

الاقتصاد السوري بين «المطرقة» و«السندان»
بقلم المحامي الأستاذ نذير سنان   ص٥-٧

الـمُفْرَدات Vocabulary 🔊

Vocabulary items are listed in alphabetical order. Nouns are followed by their plurals after the letter ج for جَمْع "plural," and verbs are listed in the past-tense third-person masculine singular form, followed by the present-tense form in parentheses and the verbal noun after the parentheses. Nouns starting with the definite article are listed according to the first letter of the word. Transliteration is given for those words containing letters with which you are currently unfamiliar. Listen to the vocabulary items on the CD and practice their pronunciation.

proper noun (man's name) . . . . (n., m.) أَديب

name *ism* . . . . (n., m.) اِسْم ج أَسْماء

good-bye (*ilā lliqā'*) . . . . إلى اللِقاء

name of the letter *alif* . . . . (n., f.) أَلِف

may God keep you safe . . . . الله يُسَلِّمُك

I . . . . (pron.) أنا

hello, welcome (*'ahlan*) (response to a greeting) . . . . . أَهْلاً

also (*ayḍan*) . . . . أَيْضاً

pleased to meet you (*tašarrafnā*) . . . . تَشَرَّفْنا
(literally: "we've been honored")

name of the letter *dāl* . . . . (n., f.) دال

name of the letter *ḏāl* . . . . (n., f.) ذال

name of the letter *rā'* . . . . (n., f.) راء

name of the letter *zāy* . . . . (n., f.) زاي

peace be upon you . . . . السَلامُ عَلَيْكُمْ
(*as-salāmu 'alaykum*) (greeting)

furṣa sa'īda . . . . فُرْصة سَعيدة
(literally: happy opportunity = pleased to meet you)

hello (*marḥaban*) (greeting) . . . . مَرحَباً

good evening (*masā' al-khayr*) (greeting) . . . . . مَساء الخَيْر

good evening (*masā' al-nūr*) (response). . . . . . . مَساء النور

good-bye (*ma'a s-salāma*) . . . . مَعَ السَلامَة

name of the letter *wāw* . . . . (n., f.) واو

wa 'alaykumu s-salām. . . . . وَعَلَيْكُمُ السَلام
(response to *as-salāmu 'alaykum*)

بِسمِ اللهِ الرَحمنِ الرَحيم

An ornate calligraphic representation of the Arabic phrase
"In the Name of God the Compassionate the Merciful"

الوَحدَةُ الثانِيةُ

Unit Two

Objectives

- Identifying yourself and others
- Introduction to separate personal pronouns
- Introduction to the two-way connectors ب ت ث ن ي
- Introduction to the long and short vowels

---

1. Identifying Yourself and Others 🔊 AUDIO

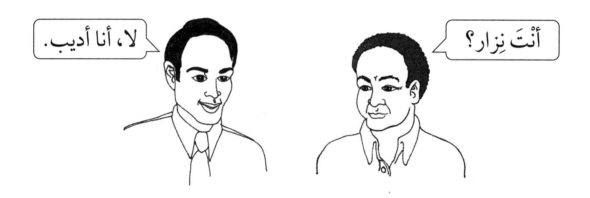

Exchange 1

In Unit 1 we learned how to introduce ourselves by saying *anā* أنا "I" plus our name. As you can see in Exchange 1, we can identify the person we are talking to by using *anta* أَنْتَ "you" (masculine) or, as in Exchange 2 on the following page, *anti* أَنْتِ "you" (feminine) and that person's name.

It should be noted that we can introduce or identify a person not present (third person) by using *huwa* هُوَ "he" and *hiya* هِيَ "she" plus that person's name.

Bear in mind that the exchanges in the drawings above and below proceed from right to left.

Exchange 2

In Exchange 1, the man responds using the word ‫ ﻻ‬ *lā*. Can you guess its meaning from context? In Exchange 2, the woman indeed is Hala, hence she replies using the word ‫ﻧَﻌَﻢ‬ *na'am*. Again, try to figure out the meaning from the context.

Inquiring about Someone's Name

When we want to ask about someone's name, we simply say the question particle ‫ ﻣﺎ‬ *mā* followed by the word ‫ اﺳﻢ‬ *ism*, which we learned means "name." To this word, we have to add an attached pronoun, which differs with gender. We are going to limit our questions for right now to just the feminine singular and masculine singular forms of "you." Listen and repeat during the pause:

When asking a man his name, use	‫ﻣﺎ اﺳْﻤُﻚَ؟‬
When asking a woman her name, use	‫ﻣﺎ اﺳْﻤُﻚِ؟‬

تمرين ١

Conversation: In groups of three, greet your fellow classmates by either guessing their name (as in Exchanges 1 and 2) or by asking them their name in the manner described in section A. The person responding must respond appropriately in either situation. After that, say good-bye. At the end of this exercise, groups should report their findings in third person by introducing their group to the class (e.g., "he is John; she is Mary").

 تمرين ٢

Listen and respond: Listen to the prompts and respond appropriately during the pauses. After listening to the exercise, fill in the blanks with your responses in transliteration (i.e., Latin script).

1–	*as-salāmu 'alaykum.*	السَلامُ عليكُم.	١–
2–			٢–
1–	*mā smuka / mā smuki?*	ما اسْمُكَ؟ / ما اسْمُكِ؟	١–
2–			٢–
1–	*tašarrafnā.*	تَشَرَّفْنا.	١–
2–			٢–
1–	*ilā lliqā'.*	إلى اللِقاءِ.	١–
2–			٢–

2. Separate Personal Pronouns

The words you have used to introduce and identify yourself and others are called **personal pronouns**. So far, we have covered five singular pronouns (as illustrated in the table on the following page). You will notice that Arabic distinguishes between masculine (m.) and feminine (f.) in second-person pronouns (you).

Separate Singular Personal Pronouns		
Pronunciation	Meaning	Pronoun
anā	I	أَنا
anta	you (m.)	أَنْتَ
anti	you (f.)	أَنْتِ
huwa	he	هُوَ
hiya	she	هِيَ

تمرين ٣

Listen and recognize: Listen to the utterances and determine whom the speaker is identifying. Mark your choice by checking the appropriate box, as in the example.

Third person (m.)	Third person (f.)	Addressee (m.)	Addressee (f.)	Self	
☐	☐	☑	☐	☐	مِثال:
☐	☐	☐	☐	☐	١–
☐	☐	☐	☐	☐	٢–
☐	☐	☐	☐	☐	٣–
☐	☐	☐	☐	☐	٤–
☐	☐	☐	☐	☐	٥–
☐	☐	☐	☐	☐	٦–

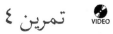

تمرين ٤

DVD: Watch Unit 2. When you are watching the DVD, become an active participant by repeating what you hear, trying to imitate the sounds and inflections used in the scenes.

Dialogue 1: Circle the best choice:

1. What is the name of Speaker 2?

    a.   Ayman
    b.   Sami
    c.   Nour
    d.   Ahmad

2. How did Speaker 1 say "excuse me"?

    a.   *masā' al-khayr*
    b.   *'afwan*
    c.   *furṣa saʿīda*
    d.   *masā' al-nūr*

Dialogue 2: Circle the best choice:

1. What are the names of the two speakers?

a.	Name of Speaker 1	b.	Name of Speaker 2
	Hala		Manal
	Rana		Shukran
	Muna		Rafiqa
	Manal		Hala

2. How did Speaker 1 say "thank you" to Speaker 2?

    a.   *naʿam*
    b.   *šukran*
    c.   *tašarrafnā*

3. Arabic Alphabet: Two-Way Connectors

ي   ن   ث   ت   ب

In Unit 1, we covered the letters of the alphabet that only connect to preceding letters, known as one-way connectors. The remaining letters of the Arabic alphabet are two-way connectors; that is, they connect both to preceding and following letters. Because of this feature, each letter may have up to four different forms (i.e., initial, medial, final, and independent) depending on its position in the word.

The five letters selected for this section are grouped together because in the initial and medial positions they look the same and differ in only the number and placement of dots, as you can see in the table directly below.

Forms of Some Two-Way Connectors					
Symbol	**Name**	**Independent**	**Final connected**	**Medial**	**Initial**
b	*bā'*	ب	ـب	ـبـ	بـ
t	*tā'*	ت	ـت	ـتـ	تـ
t̲	*t̲ā'*	ث	ـث	ـثـ	ثـ
n	*nūn*	ن	ـن	ـنـ	نـ
ī/y	*yā'*	ي	ـي	ـيـ	يـ

Note that in the independent and final positions, the first three letters, *bā'* (ب), *tā'* (ت), and *t̲ā'* (ث), share the same shape. The other two letters, *yā'* (ي) and *nūn* (ن), have different shapes in their independent and final positions, but similar shells in their initial and medial positions.

Also note that the initial form of a letter is used in the middle of words following a one-way connector, as in دابو where ب assumes an initial form after *alif* (ا), which is a one-way connector.

Mnemonic Devices for Remembering the Letters	

- The ب has the dot *below* its shell and the word "<u>b</u>elow" starts with the sound "b."

- The letter ت has *two* dots above its shell and the word "<u>t</u>wo" starts with the sound "t."

- The letter ث has *three* dots above its shell and the word "<u>t</u>hree" starts with the sound "<u>t</u>."

A. The Letters *bā'* (ب), *tā'* (ت), *t̲ā'* (ث) and Their Sounds

These letters share one basic shell and are differentiated by the number of dots and their placement.

t̲ā'	*tā'*	*bā'*
ثـ	تـ	بـ

Drawing the shell:

The Independent *bā'*		
Add the dot below the shell	**Go around**	**Start above the line**
بـ	⟲	↓

تمرين ٥

Trace over the gray letters: The letters appear in their initial, medial, final, and independent positions:

بِنت   جَبَل   دُبّ   باب

تاج   كِتاب   بَيْت   توت

ثَلْج   كَثيب   ثلاثَة   مِحْراث

تمرين ٦

Drawing letters: Write the following letters in their <u>initial</u>, <u>medial</u>, and <u>final</u> positions by writing the letter in groups of three, as in the example. Write as many groups as will fit on the line.

Example: بيب

ب
_____

ت
_____

ث
_____

تمرين ٧ 🔊 AUDIO

Tracing: Listen to the following words as you read them and repeat each one during the pause. Then trace over the light-toned words. Remember to proceed from right to left.

تَرْتيب   تُراث   ثابِت   ذَباب   نَبات

تَرْتيب   تُراث   ثابِت   ذَباب   نَبات

تَرْتيب   تُراث   ثابِت   ذَباب   نَبات

تمرين ٨

Forming words: See how many times you can write the same word on each line.

نَبات
_____

ذُباب
_____

ثابِت
_____

تُرَاث
_____

تَرتيب
_____

B. The Letters *nūn* (ن) and *yā'* (ي)

As you can see in the table titled **Forms of Some Two-Way Connectors** on page 25 of this unit, the shapes of the letters ي and ن differ from the others in this group in that their shells descend below the line in the independent and final positions.

yā'	*nūn*
ي	ن

Drawing the shell:

The Independent *nūn*		
Add the dot	**Go around**	**Start above the line**
ن		

The Independent *yā'*			
Add the dots	**Loop back just above the line**	**Go around**	**Start above the line**
ي			

تمرين ٩

Trace over the gray letters: The letters appear in their initial, medial, final, and independent positions:

لُبْنان　قُطْن　فَنّان　نَظّارة

قَوِيّ　رِياضِيّ　بَيْت　ياسَمين

- **Writing tip:** The *yā'* often gives beginning learners problems because they tend to write it in its independent form in the initial and medial positions. Try to remember that this grouping (i.e., ب ت ث ن ي) shares the same shell in their initial and medial forms, differing only in number and placement of the dots.

Drawing letters: Write the following letters in their <u>initial</u>, <u>medial</u>, and <u>final</u> positions by writing the letter in groups of three. Write as many groups as will fit on the line.

Example: ببب

ن

_____

ي

_____

تمرين ١١ 🔊 AUDIO

Tracing: Listen to the following words as you read them and repeat each one during the pause. Then trace over the light-toned words. Remember to proceed from right to left.

يَناير	دُيون	وادي	نادِر	ناوي
يَناير	دُيون	وادي	نادِر	ناوي
يَناير	دُيون	وادي	نادِر	ناوي

تمرين ١٢

Forming words: See how many times you can write the same word on each line.

يَناير _____

دُيون _____

وادي _____

نادِر _____

ناوي _____

Spelling: Combine the letters in each set to form words, as in the example. Do not forget to copy the short vowels. Remember that one-way connectors connect to two-way connectors only from the right side.

مِثال: ث + ر + ي + د = ثَريد _____

١- ن + ر + ي + د = _____

٢- ز + بَ + يْ + د + ي = _____

٣- رَ + ت + ي + ب = _____

٤- ي + ا + ب + ا + ن = _____

٥- بُ + د + و + ر = _____

٦- ث + ا + ب + ت = _____

٧- بَ + و + ا + دَ + ر = _____

٨- نَ + ب + ا + ت = _____

٩- وَ + ز + ي + ر = _____

١٠- ن + ا + د + ر = _____

١١- تُ + ر + اَ + ث = _____

١٢- رَ + ذ + ا + ذ = _____

١٣- و + ا + د + ي = _____

١٤- ب + ا + ت + و + ا = _____

C. The Letter *yā'* (ي) as a Vowel and a Semivowel

As you recall, the letter *wāw* (و) has two values: a long vowel (*ū*) and a semivowel (*w*). The same thing is true of the letter *yā'* (ي): it functions as a long vowel (*ī*, as in "feel") and as a semivowel (*y*, as in "yet"). As a semivowel, it has a consonantal value, which allows a short vowel to follow it. Thus, the letter *yā'* (ي) followed by any long or short vowels should automatically be interpreted as a semivowel with a consonantal value.

D. Different Handwriting Styles

The letters you have been imitating and copying are used for printing. There is a special style called *ruq'a*, used for writing notes and letters. Although handwriting varies widely in any language, Arabic script, whether handwritten or printed, follows certain conventions shared by both varieties. Note, however, that in handwriting the two dots above the *tā'* and below the *yā'* are usually replaced with a short horizontal stroke (a dash), and the three dots above the (ث) are replaced with a caret, which is a small angle facing downwards (^). Other than that, only slight variations exist. Examine these handwritten words:

سبع سنوات

4. Long and Short Vowels

The Arabic alphabet has three long vowels. We covered two of them in Unit 1 (ا and و). The third one is the vowel *yā'* (ي), which is equivalent to the vowel sound in "deed." For each of these three long vowels, there are short vowel counterparts, which are pronounced roughly half as long. Short vowels, however, are not represented by letters like long vowels. Rather, they are represented by diacritics, or signs, placed above or below the consonants they follow.

A. Vowel Length

Just as in English, vowel length in Arabic is distinctive. That is, sometimes the only difference in the pronunciation of two words is vowel length. An example in English is "deed" and "did."

In Arabic, the same process applies. The verbs for "he wrote" كَتَبَ *kataba* and "he corresponded" كَاتَبَ *kātaba* are distinguished by the length of the first vowel:

كَتَبَ *kataba*   كَاتَبَ *kātaba*

B. The Short Vowel *fatḥa* (◌َ)

The first short vowel we introduce here is called *fatḥa*. It is represented by a short slanting stroke placed above the letter it follows (e.g., دَ). The difference between a *fatḥa* and an *alif* (ا) is that the *alif* is pronounced roughly twice as long. Listen to these three consonants followed by a short then long vowel:

زَا *zā*   زَ *za*   رَا *rā*   رَ *ra*   دَا *dā*   دَ *da*

C. The Short Vowel *ḍamma* (◌ُ)

The second short vowel is called *ḍamma*. It is the short counterpart of the long vowel *wāw* و [ū] and is written above the consonant it follows. It looks like a tiny raised *wāw* (e.g., دُ). The difference between *ḍamma* and *wāw* is roughly similar to the difference between "foot" and "food" or "sun" and "soon."

زو *zū*   زُ *zu*   رو *rū*   رُ *ru*   دو *dū*   دُ *du*

D. The Short Vowel *kasra* (ِ)

The third short vowel is called *kasra*. It is represented by a short slanting stroke placed below the letter it follows (e.g., دِ). Its long counterpart is the vowel *yā'* (ي). The difference between the two is similar to that between the vowels in "dip" and "deep." Examine and pronounce the three pairs of syllables.

zī زي	zi زِ	rī ري	ri رِ	dī دي	di دِ

تمرين ١٤

Listen and repeat: Read the following words as you listen to them and repeat them during the pauses. Move from right to left. There are two items on each line:

٢- نُذور		١- رَتيب
٤- ثَرو		٣- ثابت
٦- ثِياب		٥- زِرْياب
٨- بَنان		٧- يَدان

تمرين ١٥

Listen and recognize: Listen to each word and indicate whether it contains a long or a short vowel by checking the appropriate box, as in the example.

	Long Vowel	Short Vowel
مِثال:	☑	☐
١-	☐	☐
٢-	☐	☐
٣-	☐	☐
٤-	☐	☐
٥-	☐	☐
٦-	☐	☐
٧-	☐	☐
٨-	☐	☐

Listen and recognize: Listen to the words and check the appropriate box next to the word you hear:

دانِي ☐		☐ دَنِي	١-
بارُود ☐		☐ بَرُود	٢-
رُبِي ☐		☐ رُوبِي	٣-
دَرِي ☐		☐ دَارِي	٤-
ثُوبُور ☐		☐ ثُبُور	٥-
نادِر ☐		☐ نَدِير	٦-
بَرِيد ☐		☐ بارِد	٧-
رابَب ☐		☐ رَبَاب	٨-

تمرين ١٧ 🔊
AUDIO

Dictation: Listen carefully to the words and write them down in the blank spaces below. Each word will be read twice.

٢- _____		١- _____
٤- _____		٣- _____
٦- _____		٥- _____
٨- _____		٧- _____
١٠- _____		٩- _____
١٢- _____		١١- _____
١٤- _____		١٣- _____

SUMMARY

1. Common greetings and leave-taking are exchanges made up of a phrase and an appropriate response.

2. Arabic personal pronouns distinguish between masculine and feminine in the second person (you).

3. There are 28 letters in the Arabic alphabet in addition to the *hamza* and two variants of existing letters. Six of the letters connect only to preceding letters; hence, they are called *one-way connectors*. The rest connect both to preceding and following letters. The latter group has different shapes depending on the position of the letter in a word.

4. In the Arabic sound system, there are three long vowels represented by the letters ا, و, and ي and three short vowels, which are counterparts of the long vowels, represented by diacritical marks placed above and below the letters they follow: the *fatḥa* (´), the *ḍamma* (ُ), and the *kasra* ( ).

تمرين ١٨

Letter identification: Examine this map and these two excerpts from Arabic print media and try to identify the letters ب ت ث ن ي in all word positions by circling them.

عملية السلام تتعثر في واشنطن لكن الأمريكيين متفائلون بالنتائج.

قام وزير الدولة الإيراني بزيارة ثانية إلى تونس في هذا الشهر.

الْمُفْرَدات Vocabulary 🔊

Listen to the vocabulary items on the CD and practice their pronunciation. Transliteration is given for those words containing letters with which you are currently unfamiliar.

proper noun (man's name) . . . . (n., m.) أَديب

you (m. sg.) . . . . (pron., m.) أَنْتَ

you (f. sg.) . . . . (pron., f.) أَنْتِ

proper noun (man's name) (*ayman*) . . . . . . (n., m.) أَيْمَن

name of the letter *bā'* . . . . (n., f.) باء

name of the letter *tā'* . . . . (n., f.) تاء

name of the letter *ṯā'* . . . . (n., f.) ثاء

proper noun (woman's name) . . . . (n., f.) رَنا

proper noun (man's name) (*sāmī*) . . . . . (n., m.) سامي

thank you (*šukran*) . . . . شُكْراً

excuse me; pardon; . . . . عَفْواً
you're welcome (as a response to شُكْراً)

no . . . . (negative particle) لا

proper noun (woman's name) (*manāl*) . . . . .(n., f.) مَنال

proper noun (man's name) . . . . (n., m.) نِزار

yes . . . . (particle) نَعَم

name of the letter *nūn* . . . . (n., f.) نون

proper noun (woman's name) (*hāla*) . . . . . . (n., f.) هالة

he . . . . (pron., m.) هُوَ

she . . . . (pron., f.) هِيَ

name of the letter *yā'* . . . . (n., f.) ياء

بسم الله الرحمن الرحيم

Calligraphic representation of the phrase
"In the name of God the Benevolent the Merciful"

الوَحدَةُ الثالِثةُ

Unit Three

Objectives

- Greeting someone in the morning
- Asking about well-being
- Introduction to the two-way connectors س ش ج ح خ ف ق ة

1. The Morning Greeting 🔊 AUDIO

صَباحُ النور.

صَباحُ الخَيرِ.

Exchange 1

The morning greeting *ṣabāḥu l-ḳayr* has the same function as its English counterpart. You may respond to this greeting using the same phrase (= *ṣabāḥu l-ḳayr*) or another one (e.g., *ṣabāḥu n-nūr*), just as the man does in the drawing. You will notice that these two phrases use the same first word *ṣabāḥ* (= morning), but a different second word. *al-ḳayr* can be roughly translated as "the goodness," while *an-nūr* means "the light." Listen to the recorded material and repeat these phrases for oral practice.

2. Asking about Well-Being 🔊

■ **Cultural Note:** Usually, when two people greet each other, they also ask about each other's well-being by saying "*kayfa l-ḥāl?*" More often than not, Arabs also ask about the well-being of the family and even the extended family. The culturally appropriate response is a positive one. That is, one is not expected to complain even if one is not faring well. The initial response الحَمْدُ لله بخَيْر *al-ḥamdu li-llāh bi-ḳayr* literally means "Thank God, I'm well." Later in the conversation, it is all right to express dejection or complain about an ailment. Many people, however, hedge their complaints by the phrase الشَكْوى لله *aš-šakwā li-llāh*, which loosely translated means "I complain to God." The man in the picture does not seem to be very happy, yet he uses the appropriate response.

Here are some possible responses to the question "how are you?" You can use the phrase *mā akhbāruka* (m. sg.) or *mā akhbāruki* (f. sg.) (= what's your news?) as another way to ask how someone is doing. The following responses are appropriate for either question:

	Possible Responses to كَيْفَ الحال		
Meaning	**Transliteration**	**Responses**	**Question**
perfect	*tamām*	تَمام	
well, thank God	*bi-ḳayr wal-ḥamdu li-llāh*	بِخَيْر والحَمْدُ لله	
good	*jayyid*	جَيِّد	كَيْفَ الحال؟
not bad	*lā ba's*	لا بَأْس	
tired/under the weather	*ta'bān*	تَعْبان	

تمرين ١

DVD: Watch Unit 3. When you are watching the DVD, become an active participant by repeating what you hear, trying to imitate the sounds and inflections used in the scenes.

Dialogue 1: Circle the best choice:

1. How is Speaker 1 doing?

   a.   good
   b.   not bad
   c.   thank God, well
   d.   happy

2. How is Speaker 2 doing?

   a.   tired
   b.   perfect
   c.   not bad
   d.   good

Dialogue 2: Circle the best choice:

How did Speaker 1 say "what's your news"?

   a.   *al-ḥamdu li-llāh*
   b.   *akhbārī jayyida*
   c.   *mā akhbāruki*
   d.   *ahlan wa sahlan*

Dialogue 3: Circle the best choice:

How is Speaker 2 doing?

   a.   *tamām*
   b.   *taʿbān*
   c.   *lā baʾs*
   d.   *jayyid*

Listen and respond: Listen to the prompts and respond appropriately during the pauses. After listening to the exercise, fill in the blanks with your responses in transliteration (= Latin script). Remember to be creative by varying the answer to "how are you?"

1–	ṣabāḥu l-ḵayr.	صَباحُ الخَيْر.	١–
2–			٢–
1–	kayfa l-ḥāl?	كَيْفَ الحال؟	١–
2–			٢–
1–	mā smuka? (masc. = muḏakkar) / mā smuki? (fem. = mu'annaṯ)	ما اسْمُكَ؟ (مُذَكَّر = masculine) / ما اسْمُكِ؟ (مؤنَّث = feminine)	١–
2–			٢–
1–	tašarrafnā.	تَشَرَّفْنا.	١–
2–			٢–
1–	ilā al-liqā'.	إلى اللِقاء.	١–
2–			٢–

3. Arabic Alphabet: Two-Way Connectors

ة   ق   ف   خ   ح   ج   ش   س

A. The Letters *sīn* (س) and *šīn* (ش) and Their Sounds

As you may have noticed, letters are grouped by the shapes in the Arabic alphabet. Each group shares a basic form or shell. For example, the letters *sīn* س (s) and *šīn* ش (š) have the same shell, but are differentiated by the three dots placed above the *šīn* ش. The final curved portion of both shells descends below the line.

These letters pose no pronunciation problems, as their sounds are found in English as well; س is pronounced *s*, as in "Sam," and ش is pronounced *š* as in "shine." Examine their different forms in the table on the following page.

Forms of the Two-Way Connectors (س and ش)					
Symbol	Name	Independent	Final connected	Medial	Initial
s	sīn	س	ـس	ـسـ	سـ
š	šīn	ش	ـش	ـشـ	شـ

Drawing this shell:

The Independent šīn			
Add the dots	Loop back just above the line	Make three teeth	Start on the line
ﺵ			

تمرين ٣

Trace over the gray letters: The letters appear in their initial, medial, final, and independent positions:

كَراسٍ   شَمْس   اِبْتِسام   سَيّارة

قِرْش   عُش   مِشْبَك   شارع

تمرين ٤

Drawing letters: Write the following letters in their <u>initial</u>, <u>medial</u>, and <u>final</u> positions by writing the same letter in groups of three. Write as many groups as will fit on the line.

Example: ‫ببب‬.

ـــ س

ـــ ش

🔊 تمرين ٥
AUDIO

Tracing: Listen to the following words as you read them and repeat each one during the pause. Then trace over the light-toned words. Remember to proceed from right to left.

ريش	يُشير	ياسين	سَرير	شَرار
ريش	يُشير	ياسين	سَرير	شَرار
ريش	يُشير	ياسين	سَرير	شَرار

تمرين ٦

Forming words: See how many times you can write the same word on each line.

ـــ شَرار

ـــ سَرير

ـــ ياسين

ـــ يُشير

ـــ ريش

The س **and** ش **in Handwriting:** Usually, in handwriting the three dots above ش are written as a caret ^ that is placed above the basic form after writing it. Also, the three "teeth" of these letters disappear, leaving an elongated horizontal stroke, as in this example:

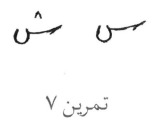

تمرين ٧

Spelling: Combine the letters in each set, including short vowels, to form words, as in the example:

مِثال: نِ + بْ + ر + ا + س   =   نِبْراس ‎_____

١-   تِ + شْ + ر + ي + ن   =   ‎_____

٢-   شَ + ر + ي + د   =   ‎_____

٣-   سَ + ي + ا + ر + ي + ن   =   ‎_____

٤-   شَ + ر + ا + ش + ي + ب   =   ‎_____

٥-   تَ + شْ + و + ي + ش   =   ‎_____

٦-   ي + ا + ب + و + س   =   ‎_____

٧-   سَ + ر + ا + ب   =   ‎_____

٨-   شَ + و + ا + رِ + ب   =   ‎_____

٩-   يُ + ش + ي + ر   =   ‎_____

١٠-   شَ + ب + ا + ب   =   ‎_____

١١-   يَ + س + ا + ر   =   ‎_____

Listen and recognize: Check the box next to the word you hear, as in the example.

مِثال: نَسيب ☑   يَشيب ☐

١-	تَشْريد ☐	تَسْديد ☐	
٢-	شَراب ☐	سَراب ☐	
٣-	روسيّ ☐	سوريّ ☐	
٤-	راس ☐	راش ☐	
٥-	شَنَب ☐	سَبَب ☐	
٦-	نَشاز ☐	ناشِز ☐	
٧-	ساري ☐	يَسار ☐	
٨-	سودان ☐	ياسين ☐	
٩-	شِرْيان ☐	شَرايين ☐	
١٠-	سار ☐	سَيْر ☐	

تمرين ٩ 🔊 AUDIO

Dictation: Listen carefully to the words you hear and write them down in the blank spaces below. Each word will be read twice.

٢- _____		١- _____	
٤- _____		٣- _____	
٦- _____		٥- _____	
٨- _____		٧- _____	
١٠- _____		٩- _____	

B. The Letters *jīm* (ج), *ḥā'* (ح), *ḳā'* (خ) and Their Sounds

As you can see, these letters share one basic shell and are differentiated by the dot and its placement.

ḳā'	*ḥā'*	*jīm*
خ	ح	ج

The table below shows the four forms of these letters in different word positions.

Forms of Some Two-Way Connectors (خ ح ج)					
Symbol	**Name**	**Independent**	**Final connected**	**Medial**	**Initial**
j	*jīm*	ج	ج	ج	ج
ḥ	*ḥā'*	ح	ح	ح	ح
ḳ	*ḳā'*	خ	خ	خ	خ

Drawing this shell:

The Independent *jīm*			
Add the dot	**Loop around**	**Go back around**	**Start above the line**
ج			

Trace over the gray letters: The letters appear in their initial, medial, final, and independent positions:

تَخَرُّج   ثَلْج   مُسَجِّلة   جامِع

فَلاَّح   بَلَح   لَحَّام   حوت

صاروخ   بِطّيخ   مَخْبَز   خاتَم

Drawing letters: Write the following letters in their <u>initial</u>, <u>medial</u>, and <u>final</u> positions by writing the same letter in groups of three. Write as many groups as will fit on the line.

Example: ‫ببب‬.

_____ ج

_____ ح

_____ خ

تمرين ١٢ 🔊 AUDIO

Tracing: Listen to the following words as you read them and repeat each one during the pause. Then trace over the light-toned words. Remember to proceed from right to left.

جِدار   تَخْدير   جَريح   زُحار   ساخِن   رَباح

جِدار   تَخْدير   جَريح   زُحار   ساخِن   رَباح

جِدار   تَخْدير   جَريح   زُحار   ساخِن   رَباح

تمرين ١٣

Forming words: See how many times you can write the same word on each line.

رَباح ـــ

ساخِن ـــ

زُحار ـــ

جَريح ـــ

تَخْدير ـــ

جِدار ـــ

تمرين ١٤

Spelling: Combine the letters in each set, including short vowels, to form words, as in the example:

مِثال: ج + ا + ر + و + ر = جارور _____

١- بِ + ا + ح + رِ = _____

٢- بِ + ا + ج + نْ + س = _____

٣- ر + ي + خ + شَ = _____

٤- س + ي + س + خَ = _____

٥- ح + ي + ب + رَ = _____

٦- ي + ر + و + ج = _____

٧- ن + و + ر + خَ + ا + س = _____

٨- ب + ا + ح + سَ = _____

٩- ن + ا + ر + ي + ج = _____

١٠- ر + ا + د + حِ + نْ + اِ = _____

Unit 3   52

1. **A Brief Phonetic Background:** Several factors contribute to how a consonant is sounded. The *first* is point of articulation. This refers to how the speech organs come into contact with one another to obstruct the flow of air in some way in order to produce a sound. The figure below titled **Organs of Speech** illustrates the speech organs and points of articulation.

Second, manner of articulation refers to the ways in which the articulation of a sound is performed. For example, a consonant may be oral (the air escapes through the mouth, as in *s*) or nasal (the air escapes through the nose, as in *m*). It may be a stop, where speech organs stop the flow of air completely and then release it explosively (e.g., *b*). A consonant may also be produced with an amount of friction when two organs come very close to each other, not stopping the air flow completely but rather allowing it to escape with friction (e.g., *s*). Fricative sounds are produced in this manner.

The *third* important factor is the state of the vocal cords. A consonant is said to be voiced if the vocal cords vibrate during its production. To experience this, place your fingers on your throat while saying *sssss* and then change to *zzzzzz*. Alternate them until you feel the difference. The first sound (*s*) is voiceless, and no vibrations in the throat can be felt, whereas the latter (*z*) is voiced, and you will feel the vibrations.

Organs of Speech

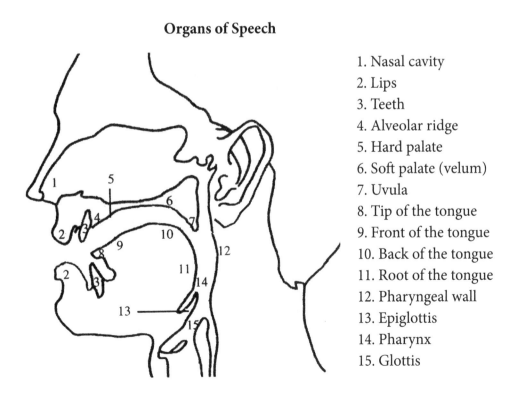

1. Nasal cavity
2. Lips
3. Teeth
4. Alveolar ridge
5. Hard palate
6. Soft palate (velum)
7. Uvula
8. Tip of the tongue
9. Front of the tongue
10. Back of the tongue
11. Root of the tongue
12. Pharyngeal wall
13. Epiglottis
14. Pharynx
15. Glottis

2. **The Sound of the Letter *jīm* (ج):** This letter is usually pronounced just like the *s* in "pleasure." Note, however, that in formal recitations (e.g., recitation of the Holy *Qur'ān*), it may be pronounced like the *j* in "judge." In parts of Egypt and Yemen it is pronounced *g* as in "gap." In colloquial speech in the Gulf area, it is pronounced *y* as in "yet." Despite these variations, the spelling remains unchanged.

3. **The Sound of the Letter *ḥā'* (ح):** The sound represented by the letter *ḥā'* ح is called by some learners of Arabic the "hard *h*," meaning that it is produced like an *h*, but with accompanying friction in the throat. There is a great deal of truth in this description. The mechanisms involved in producing the sound ح are the same used in producing the *h* sound, but with the epiglottis brought so close to the pharyngeal wall that the air escapes with friction. This consonant is voiceless; that is, no vibrations of the vocal cords occur.

4. **The Sound of the Letter *k͟hā'* (خ):** The sound represented by the letter *k͟hā'* خ is similar to the final consonants in German "Bach" and Scottish "loch." The back of the tongue lightly touches the soft palate (velum), and the air escapes with no friction. It is produced in the same place where the sharp *k* sound is produced, as you can see in the illustration below. The sound *k* is voiceless.

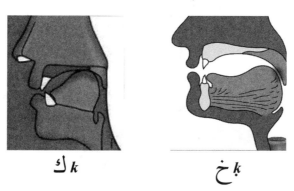

كـ *k*   خـ *k̲*

Places of Articulation of *k* and *k̲*

تمرين ١٥ 🔊

Listen and recognize: Check the box next to the word you hear, as in the example.

☐ جَري	☑ جاري	مِثال:
☐ حَرْب	☐ خَراب	١-
☐ حَرير	☐ جَرير	٢-
☐ حُدوث	☐ حَديث	٣-

حَرَش ☐	٤- جَرَش ☐
حَديد ☐	٥- جَديد ☐
تَحْرير ☐	٦- تَحْذير ☐
روخ ☐	٧- روح ☐
شَجير ☐	٨- شَخير ☐
خاسِر ☐	٩- حاسِر ☐
سَحَر ☐	١٠- ساحِر ☐

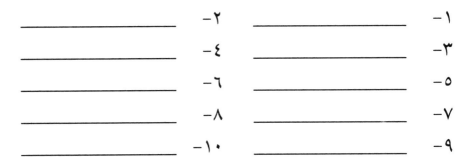

تمرين ١٦

Dictation: Listen carefully to the words you hear and write them down in the blank spaces below. Each word will be read twice.

_____ ٢-	_____ ١-
_____ ٤-	_____ ٣-
_____ ٦-	_____ ٥-
_____ ٨-	_____ ٧-
_____ ١٠-	_____ ٩-

C. The Letters *fā'* (ف) and *qāf* (ق) and Their Sounds

Although the independent shapes of these two letters are different, their shapes in the initial and medial positions resemble each other. The *qāf* ق (*q*) can be thought of as a rounder version of the letter *fā'* ف (*f*) in all positions. Possibly the most notable difference is in the independent and final positions wherein the *fā'* ف (*f*) is written flush on the line, unlike the letter *qāf* ق (*q*), which has a bowl-like shape and descends below the line.

ف ق

Forms of the Two-Way Connectors (ف and ق)					
Symbol	Name	Independent	Final connected	Medial	Initial
f	*fā'*	ف	ـف	ـفـ	فـ
q	*qāf*	ق	ـق	ـقـ	قـ

Drawing these shells:

The Independent *fā'*			
Add the dot	Make a tip	Go back around	Start above the line
ف	ق	ق	ح

The Independent *qāf*			
Add the dots	Go below the line	Make a loop	Start above the line
ق	ق	ق	ح

تمرين ١٧

Trace over the gray letters: The letters appear in their initial, medial, final, and independent positions:

خَروف   صَفّ   مِفْتاح   فَرَس

قَمَر   بَقَرة   حَلَقَ   سِباق

🔊 AUDIO   تمرين ١٨

Tracing: Listen to the following words as you read them and repeat each one during the pause, then trace over the light-toned words. Remember to proceed from right to left.

قَريب   فَريد   شُروق   فُنْدُق   رَقيق   خَفيف

قَريب   فَريد   شُروق   فُنْدُق   رَقيق   خَفيف

قَريب   فَريد   شُروق   فُنْدُق   رَقيق   خَفيف

تمرين ١٩

Forming words: See how many times you can write the same word on each line.

خَفيف
_____

رَقيق
_____

شُروق
_____

فُنْدُق
_____

فَريد
_____

قَريب
_____

تمرين ٢٠

Spelling: Combine the letters in each set, including short vowels, to form words.

_____	=	رَ + ق + ي + ب ١-
_____	تَ + ق + ا + ر + ي + ر = ٢-
_____	=	فُ + ن + و + ن ٣-
_____	=	ث + ا + قِ + ب ٤-
_____	=	فُ + ر + ا + ت ٥-
_____	=	نُ + ق + و + د ٦-
_____	=	شَ + ف + ي + ق ٧-
_____	=	س + ا + رِ + ق ٨-
_____	=	قَ + ر + ي + ب ٩-
_____	=	شُ + ر + و + ق ١٠-
_____	=	قِ + ر + ْش ١١-
_____	=	فِ + رْ + دَ + وْ + س ١٢-

1. **Phonetic Description of the *fā'* (ف):** The sound represented by the letter *fā'* ف is the same as the English *f*.

2. **Phonetic Description of the *qāf* (ق):** The sound represented by the letter *qāf* ق is slightly similar to the *k* sound in "cot," but with the back of the tongue touching the uvula (see the two illustrations on the following page). This means that its point of articulation is further back than that of *k*. You may feel the difference between the two places of articulation if you alternate pronouncing "cot" and "cat." But remember that the place of articulation of *qāf* is further back in the throat than its English counterpart. Also, the vowels (*a* and *ā*) that follow *qāf* differ in quality from the same ones when they follow *kāf* (see Unit 5). After *q*, the vowel *ā* is pronounced like the vowel in "far," whereas following *k*, it is pronounced like the vowel in "dad."

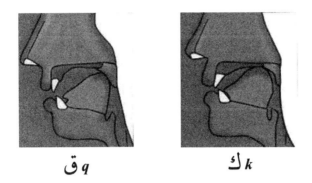

q ق k كـ

Places of Articulation of *qāf* and *kāf*

٢١ تمرين

Listen and recognize: Check the box next to the word you hear, as in the example.

فَريق ☐	رَفيق ☑	مِثال:
سَحيق ☐	سَخيف ☐	١-
ثِقاب ☐	ثُقْب ☐	٢-
قَذايف ☐	فَنادِق ☐	٣-
أَفْراخ ☐	أَفْراح ☐	٤-
رِفاق ☐	رافِق ☐	٥-
فاسِق ☐	فُسْتُق ☐	٦-
فَراديس ☐	فِردَوْس ☐	٧-
اِخْتِراق ☐	اِخْتِراف ☐	٨-
سَقَر ☐	سَفَر ☐	٩-
شُروح ☐	شُروخ ☐	١٠-

D. The Letter *tā' marbūṭa* (ة) and Its Sound

The letter *tā' marbūṭa* (ة) is a variant of the regular *tā'* (ت). It serves only as a suffix. The function for which it is best known is the feminine noun marker—meaning that when this letter is attached to most masculine nouns and adjectives, it makes them feminine.

The *tā' marbūṭa* is not always pronounced. Whether it is pronounced or not depends on the grammatical function of the word to which it is suffixed and on its structure. If the word is said by itself or is followed by an adjective, then the *tā' marbūṭa* is not pronounced. If a personal pronoun or some other suffix is attached to the word, or if the word forms a special relationship of belonging with the following noun (*iḍāfa*), then it must be pronounced just like a regular *tā'* ت.

The position of a *tā' marbūṭa* is at the end of a word. There are only two forms: (1) one connected to a preceding two-way connector; and (2) one after a one-way connector. The way to draw the two forms of this letter is illustrated in the two tables below.

ة

Unconnected

ـة

Connected

The Connected *tā' marbūṭa*			
Add the dots	**Tuck it in**	**Make a peak**	**Start on the line**
ـة			

The Unconnected *tā' marbūṭa*		
Add the dots	**Bring it up**	**Make a pear shape**
ة		

تمرين ٢٢

Trace the gray letters: The *tā' marbūṭa* appears in its connected and unconnected forms.

مَدْرَسة

صَلاة

تمرين ٢٣ 🔊 AUDIO

Tracing: Listen to the following words as you read them and repeat each one during the pause, then trace over the light-toned words. Remember to proceed from right to left.

رَبْوَة   فَرْحَة   قِيادَة   سورية   نُسَيْبَة   سارَة

رَبْوَة   فَرْحَة   قِيادَة   سورية   نُسَيْبَة   سارَة

رَبْوَة   فَرْحَة   قِيادَة   سوريّة   نُسَيْبَة   سارَة

تمرين ٢٤

Forming words: See how many times you can write the same word on each line.

سارَة
_____

نُسَيْبَة
_____

سوريّة
_____

قِيادَة
_____

فَرْحَة
_____

رَبْوة
_____

Attaching a Suffix to a Word Ending in ة: If a suffix is attached to a word ending in a *tā' marbūṭa*, this letter assumes the medial shape of a regular *tā'*, as in: (قَرْيَة + ي) قَرْيَتي and جَريدَتي (جَريدة + ي). In these two cases, the possessive pronoun ي "my" has been attached to a feminine word; thus the *tā' marbūṭa* has taken the shape of a medial *tā'*, as illustrated in the table below.

The *tā' marbūṭa* after a Suffix is Added	
Following a one-way connector:	Following a two-way connector:
(ة) جَريدَة + ي = جَريدَتي	(ـة) قَرْيَة + ي = قَرْيَتي

Spelling: Combine the letters in each set, including short vowels, to form words. Remember to change ة into a regular ت if a suffix follows, as in the example:

شُرْبَتي	=	مِثال: شُ + رْ + بَ + ة + ي
_____	=	١- خَ + شْ + يَ + ة + ي
_____	=	٢- جَ + ر + ي + دَ + ة + ي
_____	=	٣- دَ + ف + ي + نَ + ة
_____	=	٤- شَ + ر + ي + فَ + ة
_____	=	٥- ح + ا + رِ + سَ + ة
_____	=	٦- قَ + ا + ر + و + رَ + ة + ي
_____	=	٧- ز + ي + ا + رَ + ة + ي
_____	=	٨- حَ + ق + ي + بَ + ة + ي
_____	=	٩- فَ + خْ + رَ + ة
_____	=	١٠- سَ + ف + ي + نَ + ة + ي

Dictation: Write down the six words dictated to you. Each word will be read twice. Note that words ending in *tā' marbūṭa* not followed by a suffix or another noun are pronounced simply with a final short *a* (*fatḥa*) with a silent *t*. The word خَبيرَة, for example, is pronounced *kabīra* with no *t* sound on the end.

_____	٢-	_____	١-
_____	٤-	_____	٣-
_____	٦-	_____	٥-

Identification: Identify the letters س ش ج ح خ ف ق ة in these excerpts from Arabic newspapers and the game cover (on the following page) by circling them.

آخِرُ خَبَرٍ
سَتَبْدَأُ غَداً الأَحَدَ أَعْمالُ الدَّوْرَةِ التَّدْريبِيَّةِ لِلإعلام
الزِراعِيِّ والَّتي تُقامُ بِرِعايَةِ السَّيِّدِ خَليل عَرنوقَ
وَزيرِ الزِراعَة.

حَرَكَةُ القِطارات
مِن دِمَشْقَ مُباشَرَةً دونَ تَوَقُّفٍ إلى حَلَبَ ١٦،١٠
مِن دِمَشْقَ إلى حِمْصَ، حَماةَ، حَلَب الرَقَّةَ دَيْر
الزَوْر الحَسَكَةِ القامِشلي ١٧،٢٥ إلى طَرطوس
وَاللاذِقِيَّة ٠،٣١.

Quraish Game® is a registered trademark of AfkarMedia ltd.
Created by Radwan Kasmiya. All rights reserved. www.afkarmedia.com

الْمُفْرَدات 🔊

Listen to the vocabulary items on the CD and practice their pronunciation. Transliteration is given for those words containing letters with which you are currently unfamiliar.

fine, well	بِخَيْر
tired (ta'ban)	تَعْبان
perfect; great (tamām)	تَمام
good	جَيِّد
name of the letter jīm (n., f.)	جيم
name of the letter ḥā' (n., f.)	حاء
condition, circumstance (n., f.) حال ج أَحْوال	
thank God, praise be to God	الحَمدُ لِلّه
(al-ḥamdu li-llāh bi-kayr)	
name of the letter kā' (n., f.)	خاء
news	خَبَر ج أَخْبار
name of the letter sīn (n., f.)	سين
name of the letter šīn (n., f.)	شين
good morning (ṣabāḥu l-kayr)	صَباحُ الخَيْر
good morning (response = ṣabāḥu n-nūr)	صَباحُ النور
name of the letter fā' (n., f.)	فاء
name of the letter qāf (n., f.)	قاف
a little bit; slightly (qalīlan)	قَليلاً
how (kayfa)	كَيفَ
how are you? (kayfa l-ḥāl?)	كَيفَ الحال؟
not bad (lā ba's)	لا بأس
what's new? what's going on? (mā akhbāruk)	ما أَخْبارُك

الوَحدَةُ الرابِعَةُ

Unit Four

Objectives

- Inquiring about and identifying place of origin
- Introduction to the subject and predicate
- Introduction to separate pronouns
- Introduction to colloquial Arabic
- Introduction to the two-way connectors ص ض ط ظ ع غ
- Inquiring about and identifying Arab cities
- Introduction to Arab states, political systems, and capitals

1. Inquiring about and Identifying Place of Origin

Exchange 1

Inquiring about and identifying place of origin is accomplished using fairly simple structures in Arabic. To ask "Where are you from?" we begin with the preposition *min* مِنْ (from), followed by the question word *ayna* أَيْنَ (where), and a personal pronoun, أنتَ or أنتِ (see examples 1 and 2 below). You should use example 1 when talking to a woman, while example 2 is used when talking to a man.

١-   مِن أَينَ أَنتِ؟

٢-   مِن أَينَ أنتَ؟

When asking where a certain person (not in present company) comes from, simply replace أنت with the correct third-person pronoun, either *huwa* هُوَ (he) or *hiya* هِيَ (she).

٣-   مِن أَينَ هُوَ/ هِيَ؟

The response to such questions begins with a personal pronoun (أنا، هُوَ، هِيَ), followed by the preposition مِن "from," and ends with the place of origin.

٤-   أنا مِن ــــــــ.

A follow-up question may involve where a town, a region, or a country is located, as in Exchange 2 below.

فاسُ في المَغْرِب.   أَينَ فاس؟

Exchange 2

You may inquire about the location of a town with a question that contains the question word أَينَ "where" plus the name of that town. The answer to this question involves the use of the name of that town, the preposition *fī* في "in," and the name of the country or state in which it is located, as in the example above.

2. Subject and Predicate

You may have noticed from the previous exchanges that there is no verb "to be" (e.g., is, are) in these structures. Let's examine the sentences more closely.

- To inquire about a woman's place of origin, you may say:

min ayna anti?	٥ مِنْ أَيْنَ أَنتِ؟

from where you (f.)? (Where are you from?)

- In order to identify your place of origin, you might say:

anā min fās	٦ أَنا مِنْ فاس.

I from Fez (I'm from Fez).

- And to inquire about the location of a town, you may ask:

ayna fās?	٧ أَيْنَ فاس؟

where Fez? (Where's Fez?)

- The answer to such a question is made up of the name of that town, the preposition في "in," and the name of the wider region:

Fās fī al-maġrib	٨ فاسُ في الْمَغْرِب.

Fez in Morocco (Fez is in Morocco.)

Clearly, there is no verb "to be" in the above sentences. Unlike English, "be" is usually not used in the present tense in Arabic. Sentences that lack the verb "to be," or that do not start with a verb, are known as *nominal sentences*—the term "nominal" refers to the word "noun." The subject (or topic of the sentence) may be a noun or a pronoun. The predicate (or the information or comment about the subject)—shown in gray boxes below—can be a noun or a prepositional phrase, as in these examples:

You are Reema.	٩ أَنْتِ ريما.
I am from Fez.	١٠ أَنا مِن فاس.

Examples 5–10 on the previous page are made up of two parts: *subject* and *predicate*. The *subject* is the focus, or topic, of the sentence, such as أنا "I" in example 6 and فاس "Fez" in example 8. The *predicate* is the information, or comment, about the subject, such as مِن فاس "from Fez" in example 6 and في المَغْرِب "in Morocco" in example 8. The table below titled **Predicate/Subject** illustrates this point.

Examples 5 and 7, on the other hand, are questions and therefore the order of the subject and predicate is reversed. Thus, أنتِ "you" (f.) in example 11 and فاس "Fez" in example 12 are subjects, and مِن أينَ "from where" and أينَ "where" are predicates.

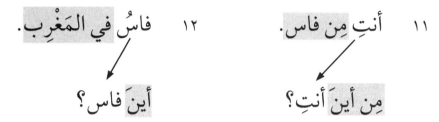

Predicate	Subject
مِن فاس	أنتِ
في المَغْرِب	فاسُ

تمرين ١ VIDEO

DVD: Watch Unit 4. When you are watching the dialogues, become an active participant by repeating what you hear, trying to imitate the sounds and inflections used in the scenes.

Dialogue 1: Circle the best choice:

1. Where is Nabil from?

    a.   Tripoli
    b.   Damascus
    c.   Baghdad
    d.   Saudi Arabia

2. Where is John from?

    a.   New York
    b.   Columbus
    c.   Wichita
    d.   Dallas

Dialogue 2: Circle the best choice:

1. Where is Rasha from?

    a.   Mauritania
    b.   Damascus
    c.   Baghdad
    d.   Fez

2. What is the name of the girl from Egypt?

    a.   Danya
    b.   Misr
    c.   Alexandria
    d.   Fas

تمرين ٢ 🔊 AUDIO

Listen and respond: Listen to the prompts and respond appropriately during the pauses. After listening to the exercise, fill in the blanks with your responses in transliteration (= Latin script).

١- السَلامُ علَيكُم.

٢- _____.

١- كَيْفَ الحال؟

٢- _____.

١- ما اسْمُكَ (مُذَكَّر) / ما اسْمُكِ (مؤنَّث)؟

٢- _____.

١- تَشَرَّفْنا.

٢- _____.

١- مِن أينَ أنتَ / أنتِ.

٢- _____.

١- أينَ _____؟

٢- _____.

١- إلى اللِقاء.

٢- _____.

تمرين ٣

Conversation: Hold a conversation in Arabic with a classmate, much like you did in Unit 2, but this time you are going to find out where your partner is from. To complete this task you must remember to (1) greet your classmate; (2) introduce yourself; (3) ask where your partner is from; (4) ask where that place is; and (5) say good-bye. Try to incorporate as many as possible of the greetings and questions that you have learned thus far. Endeavor to meet as many of your classmates as you can. Remember that the more you practice, the more fluent you become.

3. Separate Pronouns 🔊

The pronouns we have covered thus far include only those that refer to one person (singular). There are, however, some pronouns that we have not covered, such as dual form (which refers to two people) and plural (more than two people). Independent plural pronouns are gender-specific in Arabic. That is to say, we use a certain pronoun when referring to a group of women and a different pronoun when referring to a group of men. The table below titled **Separate Pronouns** lists all separate pronouns arranged according to person. Listen to the CD and repeat the pronoun during the pause. Transliteration is given for those words containing letters with which you are currently unfamiliar.

Separate Pronouns			
Person	**Pronoun**	**Meaning**	**Transliteration**
First Person	أنا	I	
	نَحنُ	we	
Second Person	أنتَ	you (m. sg.)	
	أنتِ	you (f. sg.)	
	أنتُما	you (f./m., dual)	*antumā*
	أنتُم	you (m. pl.)	*antum*
	أنتُنَّ	you (f. pl.)	
Third Person	هُوَ	he	
	هِيَ	she	
	هُما	they (f./m., dual)	*humā*
	هُم	they (m. pl.)	*hum*
	هُنَّ	they (f. pl.)	

4. Colloquial Arabic

The type of Arabic presented in this textbook is the standard language used in education, the media, and formal situations. The difference between Standard Arabic and any local colloquial Arabic is found in the pronunciation of certain letters and in certain syntactic structures. For example, the word أَينَ in this lesson is وين (wēn) or فين (fēn) in colloquial speech. Thus, one would ask وين/فين دِمَشق؟ instead of أَينَ دمشق؟. In Syrian Arabic, for example, the question مِن أَينَ أَنتِ؟ is formed as follows: مْنين إنتِ؟. Note that مِن أين (min ayna) changes into مْنين (mnēn), where the two words are collapsed into one; the first word loses the short vowel i, and the diphthong ay in the second changes to the long vowel ē.

5. Arabic Alphabet: Two-Way Connectors

A. The Letters ṣād (ص) and ḍād (ض) and Their Sounds

These two letters share one basic shape. The only difference between the two is the dot placed above the ḍād ض. Examine these letters below. They are written in one stroke, moving clockwise. The dot is placed above the letter ض after its stem is written.

Forms of the Two-Way Connectors (ص and ض)					
Symbol	**Name**	**Independent**	**Final connected**	**Medial**	**Initial**
ṣ	ṣād	ص	ـص	ـصـ	صـ
ḍ	ḍād	ض	ـض	ـضـ	ضـ

Drawing this shell:

The Independent *ḍād*			
Add the dot	Loop down and then back above the line	Wrap around and slightly above	Start just below the line
ض	ـص	ـص	ص

تمرين ٤

Trace over the gray letters: The letters appear in their initial, medial, final, and independent positions:

قُرْص   لِصّ   بَصَل   صَباح

الرِياض   تَنْهَضُ   حَضانة   ضِفْدَع

Drawing letters: Write the following letters in their <u>initial</u>, <u>medial</u>, and <u>final</u> positions by writing the same letter in groups of three. Write as many groups as will fit on the line.

Example: ‫ببب‬.

ص ————————————————————————————————————

ض ————————————————————————————————————

تمرين ٦

Tracing: Listen to the following words as you read them and repeat during the pause. Then trace over the light-toned words and copy them several times on a ruled sheet of paper.

صَبور بَصير فُرْصَة بَيْض ضَرير نُضوب

صَبور بَصير فُرْصَة بَيْض ضَرير نُضوب

صَبور بَصير فُرْصَة بَيْض ضَرير نُضوب

تمرين ٧

Forming words: See how many times you can write the same word on each line.

صَبور————————————————————————————————

بَصير————————————————————————————————

فُرْصَة————————————————————————————————

بَيْض————————————————————————————————

ضَرير————————————————————————————————

نُضوب————————————————————————————————

Spelling: Combine the letters in each set, including short vowels, to form words, as in the example:

صاروخ _____	=	مِثال: ص + ا + ر + و + خ
_____	=	١- صَ + ر + ي + ر
_____	=	٢- فُ + رَ + ص
_____	=	٣- ضَ + ف + ي + ر + ة
_____	=	٤- صُ + د + و + ر
_____	=	٥- يَ + صْ + فِ + رُ
_____	=	٦- قَ + و + ا + رِ + ض
_____	=	٧- رَ + ص + ي + ن
_____	=	٨- قَ + و + ا + نِ + ص
_____	=	٩- ح + ا + ضِ + ر
_____	=	١٠- إِ + نْ + خ + ف + ا + ض
_____	=	١١- ر + ص + ي + ف
_____	=	١٢- صَ + فَّ + ا + رَ + ة
_____	=	١٣- قُ + ضْ + ب + ا + ن
_____	=	١٤- إِ + خْ + تِ + ص + ا + ص
_____	=	١٥- أَ + بْ + ي + ض

1. **The Sound of the Letter ṣād (ص):** To your ear, at least at this stage, the sound represented by the letter *ṣād* might at first resemble the sound of *sīn* س (*s*), but in fact the two letters are produced differently. The ص sound is said to be pharyngealized. This means that the back of the tongue is raised toward the soft palate during articulation, and the front of the tongue (not tip) is lowered or hollowed, causing a change in sound quality (see the following diagrams). The Arabic sound ص is similar to the *s* in "ṣod," whereas the sound represented by the letter *sīn* س is more like the *s* in "ṣeen." Again, to your ear, the difference might be in the following vowel rather than in the consonant itself. In essence, then, Arabic has two versions of the sound *s*, one plain, or regular, and the other pharyngealized.

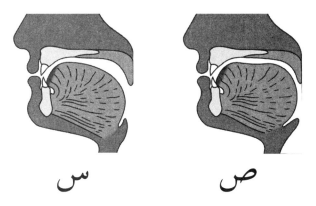

Plain (*s*) versus Pharyngealized (*ṣ*) Articulation

2. **The Sound of the Letter ḍād (ض):** The sound represented by the letter *ḍād* ض (*ḍ*) is the pharyngealized counterpart of *dāl* د (*d*) and is produced with the back of the tongue raised toward the soft palate. It sounds like the *d* in "ḍark," whereas د sounds like the *d* in "ḍad." The following diagram illustrates the difference between a pharyngealized sound and its counterpart.

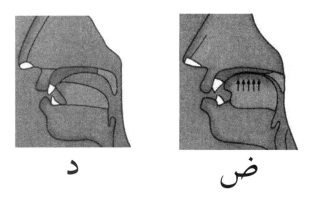

Plain (*d*) versus Pharyngealized (*ḍ*) Articulation

تمرين ٩ 🔊

Listen and recognize: Check the box next to the word you hear, as in the example.

سيرة ☐	صورة ☑	:مِثال
فَضيحة ☐	فَصيحة ☐	١-
رَسين ☐	رَصين ☐	٢-
دَجيج ☐	ضَجيج ☐	٣-
رُدود ☐	رُضوض ☐	٤-
فَريدة ☐	فَريضة ☐	٥-
ساد ☐	صاد ☐	٦-
رَسيف ☐	رَصيف ☐	٧-
داري ☐	ضاري ☐	٨-
صاري ☐	ساري ☐	٩-
يُسْرِف ☐	يَصْرِف ☐	١٠-

تمرين ١٠ 🔊

Dictation: Listen carefully to each word dictated to you and write it down in the space provided below. Each word will be read twice.

_____ ٢-	_____ ١-
_____ ٤-	_____ ٣-
_____ ٦-	_____ ٥-
_____ ٨-	_____ ٧-
_____ ١٠-	_____ ٩-

B. The Letters *ṭā'* (ط) **and** *ẓā'* (ظ) **and Their Sounds**

These two letters also share one basic form. They are distinguished by a dot placed above the loop in *ẓā'* ظ. Note that they are written flush on the line.

ظ   ط

Forms of the Two-Way Connectors (ط and ظ)					
Symbol	Name	Independent	Final connected	Medial	Initial
ṭ	ṭāʾ	ط	ـط	ـطـ	طـ
ẓ	ẓāʾ	ظ	ـظ	ـظـ	ظـ

Drawing this shell:

The Independent ẓāʾ		
Add the dot	Draw a stem from the top	Start on the line and wrap around
ظ		

تمرين ١١

Trace over the gray letters: The letters appear in their initial, medial, final, and independent positions:

وَطْواط   شَريط   خِطاب   طَالِب

إِكْتِظاظ   الحَظ   مِظَلَّة   ظِلّ

تمرين ١٢

Drawing letters: Write the following letters in their <u>initial</u>, <u>medial</u>, and <u>final</u> positions by writing the same letter in groups of three. Write as many groups as will fit on the line.

Example: .ببب

ط
_____

ظ
_____

تمرين ١٣

Tracing: Listen to the following words as you read them and repeat each one during the pause. Then trace over the light-toned words and copy them several times on a ruled sheet of paper. Remember to proceed from right to left.

قَيْظ   خُطوط   حَظيرة   خَطير   ظَريف   طَروب

قَيْظ   خُطوط   حَظيرة   خَطير   ظَريف   طَروب

قَيْظ   خُطوط   حَظيرة   خَطير   ظَريف   طَروب

تمرين ١٤

Forming words: See how many times you can write the same word on each line.

طَروب _____

ظَريف _____

خَطير _____

حَظيرة _____

خُطوط _____

قَيْظ _____

تمرين ١٥ 🔊

Spelling: Combine the letters in each set, including short vowels, to form words, as in the example:

مِثال: ض + ا + بِ + ط   =   ضابِط _____

١-   طَ + رْ + ب + و + ش   =   _____

٢-   قِ + ط + ا + ر   =   _____

٣-   ف + ظ + ا + ظ + ة   =   _____

٤-   رُ + طَ + ب   =   _____

٥-   ب + و + ص   =   _____

٦-   طَ + ر + ي + ق   =   _____

٧-   ظَ + ر + ي + ف   =   _____

٨-   بَ + س + ا + ط + ة   =   _____

٩-   خَ + ر + ي + ط + ة   =   _____

١٠-   تَ + شْ + ط + ي + ب   =   _____

Pronunciation of ط and ظ: Like ص and ض, the sounds represented by these two letters are pharyngealized. That is, the back of the tongue is raised toward the soft palate. The difference between *ṭāʾ* ت (plain *t*) and *ṭāʾ* ط (phayngealized *ṭ*) is similar to the difference between the *t* sounds in "Tim" and "Todd." While this difference is not distinctive in English, it is in Arabic. For example, the word for "mud" is طين (*ṭīn*) and the word for "figs" is تين (*tīn*). Similarly, the *ẓāʾ* is pharyngealized, while its counterpart *dāl* ذ is not. The difference between the two is similar to the difference between the *th* sounds in "<u>th</u>ine" and "<u>th</u>is," respectively.

تمرين ١٦

Listen and recognize: Check the box next to the word you hear, as in the example.

تَباشير ☐	طَباشير ☑	مِثال:	
رَطيب ☐	رَتيب ☐	١-	
طَريف ☐	ظَريف ☐	٢-	
ظافِر ☐	ذافِر ☐	٣-	
طارِق ☐	تارِك ☐	٤-	
تين ☐	طين ☐	٥-	
ظَرْف ☐	ذَرْف ☐	٦-	
أطراب ☐	أتراب ☐	٧-	
بَطَر ☐	بَتَر ☐	٨-	
نَظير ☐	نَذير ☐	٩-	
حَذَر ☐	حَظَر ☐	١٠-	

تمرين ١٧

Dictation: Listen carefully to each word dictated to you and write it down below or on a ruled sheet of paper. Each word will be read twice.

٢- _____	١- _____
٤- _____	٣- _____

ــــــــــــــــــ	٦-	ــــــــــــــــــ	٥-
ــــــــــــــــــ	٨-	ــــــــــــــــــ	٧-
ــــــــــــــــــ	١٠-	ــــــــــــــــــ	٩-

تمرين ١٨ 🔊

Recognizing the emphatic letters: Listen to the two words read to you. Check the box next to the word that most closely resembles the word's English counterpart. Notice how the emphatic letters change the sound of the *alif*. On the line next to the words, write the English cognate, as in the example.

_____water_____	☑	واطَر	☐	واتَر	مِثال:
ــــــــــــــــــ	☐	فاذَر	☐	فاظَر	١-
ــــــــــــــــــ	☐	ضاد	☐	داد	٢-
ــــــــــــــــــ	☐	قار	☐	كار	٣-
ــــــــــــــــــ	☐	طانْجَرين	☐	تانْجَرين	٤-
ــــــــــــــــــ	☐	سيصا	☐	سيسا	٥-
ــــــــــــــــــ	☐	ضاتَر	☐	داتَر	٦-
ــــــــــــــــــ	☐	شاطَر	☐	شاتَر	٧-
ــــــــــــــــــ	☐	ضاينْجَر	☐	داينْجَر	٨-

C. The Letters *'ayn* (ع) and *ġayn* (غ) and Their Sounds

These two letters share the same basic shape, although they are two different sounds. As you can see below, the basic shape in the independent position is made up of two semicircles on top of each other facing right. They are written in one uninterrupted stroke. The lower, larger segment descends below the line. The medial shape is written as an open loop flush on the line.

غ   ع

Forms of the Two-Way Connectors (ع and غ)					
Symbol	Name	Independent	Final connected	Medial	Initial
'	*'ayn*	ع	ـع	ـعـ	عـ
ġ	*ġayn*	غ	ـغ	ـغـ	غـ

Drawing these shells:

The Independent *ġayn*			
Add the dot	Complete the second loop	Retrace and start a second loop that is larger than the first	Make a loop going slightly past your starting point
غ			

The Medial *'ayn*				
Final form	Continue on your way	Complete the loop	Make the top of the triangle	From the line start making an upside-down triangle

Trace over the gray letters: The letters appear in their initial, medial, final, and independent positions:

شارِع   الربيع   بَعير   عالِم

فارِغ   تَبْغ   تَغريد   غُراب

Drawing letters: Write the following letters in their <u>initial</u>, <u>medial</u>, and <u>final</u> positions by writing the same letter in groups of three. Write as many groups as will fit on the line.

Example: ببب.

ع
غ

_____

_____

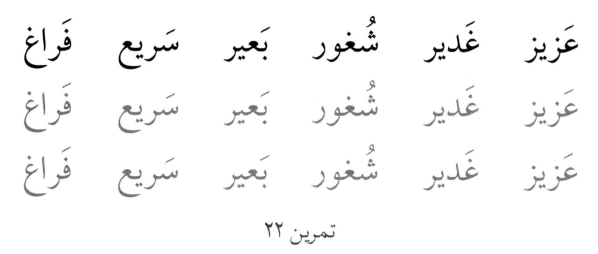

تمرين ٢١ 🔊 AUDIO

Tracing: Listen to the following words as you read them and repeat each one during the pause. Then trace over the light-toned words and copy them several times on a ruled sheet of paper. Remember to proceed from right to left.

فَراغ   سَريع   بَعير   شُغور   غَدير   عَزيز

فَراغ   سَريع   بَعير   شُغور   غَدير   عَزيز

فَراغ   سَريع   بَعير   شُغور   غَدير   عَزيز

تمرين ٢٢

Forming words: See how many times you can write the same word on each line.

عَزيز _____

غَدير _____

شُغور _____

بَعير _____

سَريع _____

فَراغ _____

تمرين ٢٣

Spelling: Combine the letters in each set, including short vowels, to form words, as in the example:

مِثال: عَ + ج + ي + ب   =   عَجيب _____

١- عَ + فْ + ر + ي + ت   =   _____

٢- شُ + غ + و + ر   =   _____

Unit 4

86

٣- د + غْ + دَ = ــــــــــــــــــــــــ

٤- ع + ي + د + بَ = ــــــــــــــــــــــــ

٥- غ + و + ب + تُ = ــــــــــــــــــــــــ

٦- ع + ي + ظ + فَ = ــــــــــــــــــــــــ

٧- غ + يْ + ر + فْ + تَ = ــــــــــــــــــــــــ

٨- ع + ١ + ط + تَ + سْ + ١ = ــــــــــــــــــــــــ

٩- ب + ي + ر + غِ = ــــــــــــــــــــــــ

١٠- غ + ١ + ب + صِ = ــــــــــــــــــــــــ

1. **The Sound of the Letter ʿayn (ع):** The sound represented by the letter ʿayn ع has the same place of articulation as that of ح (i.e., in the throat), but it is voiced; that is, the vocal cords vibrate (see Unit 3, page 53).

2. **The Sound of the Letter ġayn (غ):** The sound represented by the letter ġayn غ is the voiced counterpart of the sound represented by خ. It roughly resembles the Parisian *r*. The place of articulation is between the back of the tongue and the soft palate. The stream of air passing through the stricture creates a sound similar to that of gargling. The vocal cords should be vibrating; otherwise you produce the sound خ.

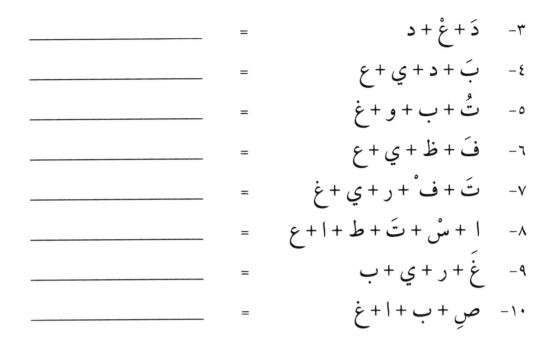

تمرين ٢٤

Listen and recognize: Check the box next to the word you hear, as in the example.

مِثال: تَغريب ☑   تَخريب ☐

١-   غَدير ☐   عَديد ☐

٢-   يَعرِف ☐   يَغرِف ☐

٣-   يُذيع ☐   يُزيغ ☐

٤-   صَبَع ☐   صَبَغ ☐

٥-   عَريف ☐   غَريق ☐

٦- بَغيض ☐ بَعيد ☐
٧- فَرَع ☐ فَرَغ ☐
٨- غَرب ☐ عَرَب ☐
٩- تَبْغ ☐ تَبِع ☐
١٠- غُراب ☐ خَراب ☐

تمرين ٢٥

Listen and recognize: Check the box next to the word you hear.

١- سَديد ☐ صَديد ☐
٢- ظَرْبان ☐ طَرْبان ☐
٣- رَديد ☐ غَديد ☐
٤- صَريع ☐ سَريع ☐
٥- صَبَر ☐ سَبَر ☐
٦- عَدوّ ☐ عُضو ☐
٧- تاب ☐ طاب ☐
٨- فَسيح ☐ فَصيح ☐

تمرين ٢٦

Transliteration: Listed in this exercise are ten names of Arab and American towns and states. Decode each one and write its English equivalent in the space provided.

٢- سوريّة _____   ١- بَيْروت _____
٤- بويزي _____   ٣- يوطا _____
٦- تونِس _____   ٥- أريزونا _____
٨- بَغْداد _____   ٧- باتُن روج _____
١٠- ويتشِطا _____   ٩- إنديانا _____

6. Inquiring about and Identifying Arab Countries

The map below illustrates the names of the countries of the Arab world. Try to add the capitals or major cities on the map.

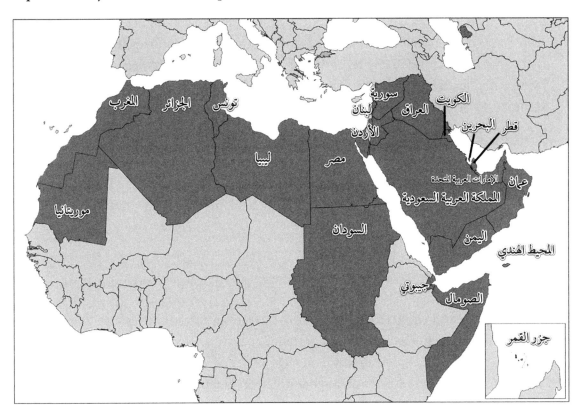

الوَطَن العَرَبيّ

Map of the Arab World

تمرين ٢٧

Conversation: For practice, form questions about locations of cities and then ask your neighbor in class. You may wish to practice at home by posing questions and answering them to yourself out loud. Answer the question using the name of that city and the country, as in the example below:

Baghdad is in Iraq. بَغْداد في العِراق. ← *Where is Baghdad?* أينَ بَغْداد؟

7. Arab States, Political Systems, and Capitals

■ **Cultural Note:** There are currently 22 Arab states that are members of the Arab League. Their combined population is about 350 million. Arab states vary in their political systems. There are republics, monarchies, and emirates. Republics are ruled by presidents, some of whom are democratically elected. Monarchies are ruled by kings who come from families that have ruled the country for centuries (e.g., Morocco) or that came to power relatively recently (e.g., Jordan). An emirate (e.g., Kuwait) is ruled by an *emir* "leader, prince." An *emir* is usually a leader of a powerful tribe or clan. He assumes the regular responsibilities of a head of state.

Arab states are developing countries. Some of them, however, have become fairly wealthy and have modernized their economies and their lifestyles. A few countries are still rather poor and underdeveloped (e.g., Somalia, Mauritania). The table in exercise 28 lists the member countries of the Arab League along with their capitals.

تمرين ٢٨

Identifying cities and countries: Look over the names of the countries and their capitals below and then circle the letters that are unfamiliar to you. Now, working with a partner and relying on the map of the Arab world on page 89, try to see how many of these countries and their capitals you can identify on a separate sheet of paper.

Capital	Country		Capital	Country	
مَسْقَط	عُمان	١٢-	عَمّان	الأُرْدُن	١-
القُدْس	فِلَسطين	١٣-	أبو ظَبي	الإمارات	٢-
الدَوْحَة	قَطَر	١٤-	المَنامة	البَحرَين	٣-
الكُوَيْت	الكُوَيْت	١٥-	تونِس	تونِس	٤-
بَيْروت	لُبْنان	١٦-	الجَزائِر	الجَزائِر	٥-
طَرابُلُس الغَرْب	ليبيا	١٧-	جيبوتي	جيبوتي	٦-
القاهِرة	مِصْر	١٨-	الرياض	السُعوديّة	٧-

Arab Countries and Their Capital Cities

الرِباط	المَغرِب	١٩-	الخُرطوم	السودان	٨-
نُواكْشوط	موريتانيا	٢٠-	دِمَشْق	سوريَّة	٩-
صَنْعاء	اليَمَن	٢١-	موقاديشو	الصومال	١٠-
موروني	جُزُر القَمَر	٢٢-	بَغداد	العِراق	١١-

تمرين ٢٩

Identify the letters: Examine these headings from Arabic print media and try to identify the letters ص ض ط ظ ع غ printed in different fonts by circling them.

تنطلق الأحد وتجمع حقائب مدرسية وتبرعات عينية

«بصمة عطاء» من مدارس الدولة لطلاب لبنان

«وطني» ينظم دورة متخصصة حول تغيير الذات في دلما

خلال مفاجآت صيف دبي

برنامج وطني ينظم ندوات اجتماعية وتربوية وصحية

100 طفل لبناني يطالبون أنان

بالتدخل لوقف العدوان

دبي - الإمارات اليوم: وقّع مئة طفل لبناني مقيمين في الدولة، بطاقة موجهة إلى الأمين العام للأمم المتحدة كوفي أنان يطالبون منه فيها التدخل الفوري لوقف الحرب في لبنان. وقالت آية صادق (10 أعوام) إن شعورا بالحزن الشديد ينتابها وهي تشاهد الأطفال والأبرياء يسقطون نتيجة هذه الحروب التي تشنها إسرائيل، وتحول لبنان.. البلد الجميل إلى دمار واسع.

وركز الأطفال في البطاقة على حق أقرانهم في لبنان في العيش بأمان، وفي أن يلهوا ويستمتعوا بحياتهم، بدلا من أن يكونوا أهدافا للقتل. ▪

Listen to the vocabulary items on the CD and practice their pronunciation. Transliteration is given for those words containing letters with which you are currently unfamiliar.

Abu Dhabi (*abū ẓabī*)	أبو ظَبي (n., f.)
Jordan (*al-urdun*)	الأردُن (n., m.)
Arizona	أريزونا (n., f.)
United Arab Emirates (*al-imārāt*)	الإمارات (n., f.)
Indiana	إندِيانا (n., f.)
where (question particle)	أيْنَ
Baton Rouge	باتِن روج (n., f.)
Bahrain (*al-baḥrayn*)	البَحرَين (n., f.)
Baghdad (*baġdād*) (capital of Iraq)	بَغْداد (n., f.)
Boise	بويزي (n., f.)
Beirut (capital of Lebanon)	بَيْروت (n., f.)
Tunis, Tunisia. . . . . (same word for capital city and country)	تونِس (n., f.)
Algiers (*al-jazā'ir*), Algeria (*al-jazā'ir*) . . . . (same word for capital city and country)	الجَزائِر (n., f.)
Djibouti (*jībūtī*)	جيبوتي (n., f.)
Khartoum (*al-ḳurṭūm*) . . . . (capital of the Sudan)	الخُرطوم (n., f.)
Damascus (*dimašq*) (capital of Syria)	دِمَشْق (n., f.)
Doha (*ad-dawḥa*) (capital of Qatar)	الدَوحة (n., f.)
Rabat (*ar-ribāṭ*) (capital of Morocco)	الرِباط (n., f.)
Riyadh (*ar-riyāḍ*) (capital of Saudi Arabia) . .	الرِياض (n., f.)
Saudi Arabia (*as-suʿūdiyya*)	السُعودية (n., f.)
the Sudan (*as-sūdān*)	السودان (n., m.)

Syria (*sūriyya*) . . . . (n., f.) سورِيَة

another name for Damascus; . . . . (n., m.) الشام
historically Greater Syria (*al-šām*)

Sanaa (*ṣanʿāʾ*) (capital of Yemen) . . . . . . (n., f.) صَنْعاء

Somalia (*aṣ-ṣōmāl*) . . . . (n., m.) الصومال

Tripoli (*ṭarābulus al-ġarb*) . . . . . . (n., f.) طَرابُلُس الغَرب
(capital of Libya)

capital . . . . (n., f.) عاصِمة ج عواصِم

Iraq (*al-ʿirāq*) . . . . (n., m.) العِراق

Arab . . . . (n., m.) عَرَبيّ ج عَرَب

Amman (*ʿammān*) (capital of Jordan) . . . . . (n., f.) عَمّان

Oman (*ʿumān*) . . . . (n., f.) عُمان

Fez (*fās*) (town in Morocco) . . . . (n., f.) فاس

Palestine (*filasṭīn*) . . . . (n., f.) فِلَسطين

in . . . . (prep.) في

Cairo (*al-qāhira*) (capital of Egypt) . . . . . (n., f.) القاهِرَة

Jerusalem (*al-quds*) (capital of Palestine) . . . (n., f.) القُدْس

Qatar (*qaṭar*) . . . . (n., f.) قَطَر

Kuwait (*al-kuwayt*) . . . . (n., f.) الكُوَيت

Lebanon (*lubnān*) . . . . (n., m.) لُبنان

Libya (*lībyā*) . . . . (n., f.) ليبيا

city . . . . (n., f.) مَدينة ج مُدُن

Muscat (*masqaṭ*) (capital of Oman) . . . . . (n., f.) مَسْقَط

Egypt (*miṣr*) . . . . (n., f.) مِصْر

Morocco (*al-maġrib*) . . . . (n., m.) المَغرِب

from, of . . . . (prep.) مِن

Manama (*al-manāma*) (capital of Bahrain) . . (n., f.) المَنامة

Mauritania (*mōritānyā*) . . . . (n., f.) موريتانيا

Mogadishu (*muqadīšō*) . . . . (n., f.) موقاديشو
(capital of Somalia)

Nouakchott (*nwakšot*) . . . . (n., f.) نواكشوط
(capital of Mauritania)

homeland . . . . (n., m.) وَطَن ج أوطان

Wichita . . . . (n., f.) ويتشِطا

Yemen (*al-yaman*) . . . . (n., m.) اليَمَن

Utah . . . . (n., f.) يوطا

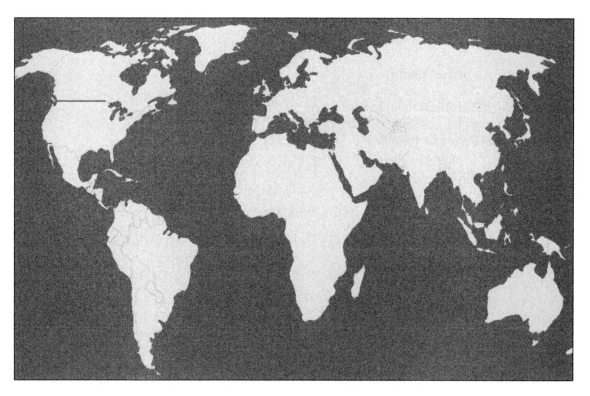

Where is the Arab World?

الوَحدَةُ الخامِسةُ

Unit Five

Objectives

- Introduction to the two-way connectors ل، ك، م، ه
- Identifying objects from the immediate environment
- Expressing possession
- Introduction to attached pronouns
- Describing national and regional affiliation
- Introduction to the relative "noun" (nisba) اِسْمُ النِسبة
- Introduction to gender in Arabic nouns

---

1. Arabic Alphabet: Two-Way Connectors

ه   م   ك   ل

A. The Letter *lām* (ل) and Its Sound

The sound of the letter *l* in Arabic is mostly light. That is to say, it is pronounced with the back of the tongue lowered and the tip touching the alveolar ridge just behind the upper teeth. By contrast, in American English, the *l* sound is usually dark, with the back of the tongue raised toward the soft palate. The word "little" has two occurrences of *l*, the first one light and the second one dark. If you can perceive the difference, it will be easy for you to pronounce the Arabic *l*, which is a light one in most cases. There are, however, instances of dark *l* in Arabic. The best-known one occurs in the word *Allah* الله "God." Also, dark *l* occurs when it precedes or follows pharyngealized sounds (e.g., ص ض ط ظ).

- Make sure not to confuse the *lām* with an *alif* in the initial and medial positions. The *lām* has a different shape in its final and independent positions. The difference between the two letters is that an *alif* is a one-way connector, whereas the *lām* is a two-way connector. Note the direction of writing the different shapes of *lām*.

ل ـل ـلـ ل

Forms of the Two-Way Connector (ل)					
Symbol	Name	Independent	Final connected	Medial	Initial
l	*lām*	ل	ـل	ـلـ	لـ

تمرين ١

Trace over the gray letters: The letters appear in their initial, medial, final, and independent positions:

سِرْوال   عَسَل   فُلَيْفِلة   لَيْمون

Important Note for the *lām-alif* Combination: When an *alif* follows a *lām*, the *alif* is written embedded inside *lām*, slanting to the right. In print, it looks like this لا when the *lām* is not connected to a preceding letter and like this ـلا when it is connected to a preceding letter. In handwriting, however, the *lām-alif* combination resembles the latter shape, as illustrated below.

أورلاندو ١٨/ ٩/ ٢٠٠٩>

أعزائي الغالين . السلام عليكم

أكتب لكم من أورلاندو . وصلت هنا منذ

ثلاثة أيام لزيارة ديزني وولد.

Tracing: Listen to the following words as you read them and repeat each one during the pause. Then trace over the light-toned words and copy them several times on a ruled sheet of paper.

لَبيب   بَليد   نِيل   نِبال   شَلَبي   الإسْلام

لَبيب   بَليد   نِيل   نِبال   شَلَبي   الإسْلام

لَبيب   بَليد   نِيل   نِبال   شَلَبي   الإسْلام

تمرين ٣

Forming words: See how many times you can write the same word on each line.

لَبيب
_____
بَليد
_____
نِيل
_____
نِبال
_____
شَلَبي
_____
الإسْلام
_____

تمرين ٤

Spelling: Combine the letters in each set, including short vowels, to form words.

_____	=	ا + لَ + يَ + ا + لَ + ل + ا ‏-١
_____	=	ل + بُ + لْ + بُ ‏-٢
_____	=	ل + سَ + عَ ‏-٣
_____	=	م + ا + ل + سْ + إِ + ل + ا ‏-٤
_____	=	ل + ا + ل + جَ ‏-٥
_____	=	ب + ي + ل + صَ ‏-٦
_____	=	ل + ا + و + نَ ‏-٧
_____	=	ة + ب + لِ + ا + ط ‏-٨
_____	=	ز + ا + ف + لْ + تِ ‏-٩
_____	=	د + ي + ل + قْ + تَ ‏-١٠
_____	=	ق + ا + ل + غْ + إِ ‏-١١

🔊 AUDIO تمرين ٥

Listen and recognize: Check the box next to the word you hear, as in the example.

☐ شِبْل	☑ سَبيل	مِثال:
☐ نَبيل	☐ بِلال	‏-١
☐ وَيْلي	☐ والي	‏-٢
☐ بلال	☐ بُلبُل	‏-٣
☐ لَدِن	☐ لادِن	‏-٤
☐ لَباب	☐ لَبيب	‏-٥
☐ بَلَدي	☐ بِلادي	‏-٦

Unit 5   98

٧- وَالِدي ☐   وَلَدي ☐

٨- لاصِق ☐   لازِق ☐

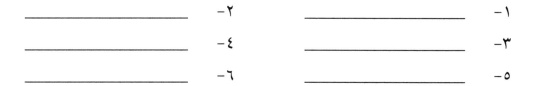

تمرين ٦ 🔊 AUDIO

Dictation: Listen to each word dictated to you and write it down below or on a ruled sheet of paper. Each word will be read twice.

٢- _____		١- _____	
٤- _____		٣- _____	
٦- _____		٥- _____	

B. The Letter *kāf* (ك) and Its Sound

The sound represented by this letter is pronounced just like the *k* in "kit."

In the independent position, it is written much like the letter *lām*, but with a flat base rather than a bowl-shaped one. Compare the letters *lām* ل and *kāf* ك in their independent position:

As you have noticed, there is a diacritical mark embedded within the *kāf*. Its function is to distinguish the *kāf* from the *lām* in the final connected and independent forms. As you can see, the diacritical mark is similar in shape to a *hamza* (see Unit 6, section 2), but it has no phonological value.

The arrows in the table on the following page show the direction you should follow when drawing ك. The table illustrates the shapes of the letter *kāf* in the other word positions.

Forms of the Two-Way Connector (ك)					
Symbol	Name	Independent	Final connected	Medial	Initial
k	*kāf*	ك اك	لك	كك	ك

تمرين ٧

Trace over the gray letters: The letters appear in their initial, medial, final, and independent positions:

شُبَّاك   سِلْك   سُكَّر   كِتاب

تمرين ٨

Tracing: Listen to the following words as you read them and repeat each one during the pause. Then trace over the light-toned words and copy them several times on a ruled sheet of paper.

سُلوك   فَلَك   تَكْبير   باكِر   كِبْريت

سُلوك   فَلَك   تَكْبير   باكِر   كِبْريت

سُلوك   فَلَك   تَكْبير   باكِر   كِبْريت

Forming words: See how many times you can write the same word on each line.

كِبْريت _____

باكِر _____

تَكْبير _____

فَلَك _____

سُلوك _____

تمرين ١٠

Spelling: Combine the letters in each set, including short vowels, to form words.

١-	كُ + رْ + د + و + س	= _____
٢-	كُ + س + و + ف	= _____
٣-	شُ + ك + و + ك	= _____
٤-	بُ + رْ + ك + ا + ن	= _____
٥-	اِ + حْ + تِ + ك + ا + ك	= _____
٦-	كَ + بْ + كَ + ب	= _____
٧-	كَ + و + ا + كِ + ب	= _____
٨-	تَ + كُ + ر + ي + ر	= _____
٩-	تَ + شْ + ك + ي + ل	= _____
١٠-	كَ + ب + ي + ر	= _____

تمرين ١١ 🔊

Listen and recognize: Check the box next to the word you hear, as in the example.

مِثال:	كَبير	☑	قُبور	☐
١-	كوت	☐	كُوَيت	☐
٢-	شاكِر	☐	شَكَر	☐
٣-	فَريك	☐	فَريق	☐
٤-	فُكوك	☐	فِكاك	☐
٥-	كاسي	☐	قاسي	☐
٦-	كَسَب	☐	كاسِب	☐
٧-	دَلَك	☐	دَلَق	☐
٨-	رَكيك	☐	رَقيق	☐
٩-	شُكوك	☐	شُقَق	☐
١٠-	قَلْب	☐	كَلْب	☐

تمرين ١٢ 🔊

Dictation: Listen to each word and write it down below. Each word will be read twice.

٢- _____	١- _____
٤- _____	٣- _____
٦- _____	٥- _____
٨- _____	٧- _____
١٠- _____	٩- _____

C. The Letter *mīm* (م) and Its Sound

The sound represented by the letter *mīm* resembles the English *m*. The table on the following page illustrates the *mīm* in its various forms.

Forms of the Two-Way Connector (م)					
Symbol	Name	Independent	Final connected	Medial	Initial
m	*mīm*	مُ	مـ	ـمـ	مـ

تمرين ١٣

Trace over the gray letters: The letters appear in their initial, medial, final, and independent positions:

نَوْم   قَلَم   جَمَل   مُدَرِّس

تمرين ١٤

Tracing: Listen to the following words as you read them and repeat each one during the pause. Then trace over the light-toned ones and copy them several times.

قَلَم	روم	كَريم	جامِعة	سَمير	مَرْيَم
قَلَم	روم	كَريم	جامِعة	سَمير	مَرْيَم
قَلَم	روم	كَريم	جامِعة	سَمير	مَرْيَم

تمرين ١٥

Forming words: See how many times you can write the same word on each line.

مَرْيَم _____

سَمير _____

جامِعة _____

كَريم _____

روم _____

قَلَم _____

تمرين ١٦

Spelling: Combine the letters in each set, including short vowels, to form words.

١- بَ + لْ + سَ + م = _____

٢- مُ + سْ + لِ + م + و + ن = _____

٣- كِ + ر + ا + م = _____

٤- مُ + ق + ي + م = _____

٥- مُ + شْ + م + ِس = _____

٦- ا + ل + مُ + د + ي + ر = _____

٧- مَ + شْ + م + و + ل = _____

٨- مَ + جْ + م + و + ع + ة = _____

٩- م + ي + ل + ا + د + ي = _____

١٠- مُ + مْ + ت + ا + ز = _____

تمرين ١٧ 🔊 AUDIO

Listen and recognize: Check the box next to the word you hear.

مُريد ☐	مُدير ☐	١-
مَسار ☐	مَيْسان ☐	٢-
دَمَس ☐	ديماس ☐	٣-
صَمَم ☐	صَميم ☐	٤-
مارِد ☐	مُراد ☐	٥-
لامِس ☐	لَميس ☐	٦-
سَلام ☐	سَليم ☐	٧-
ذِمام ☐	ذِمَم ☐	٨-

تمرين ١٨ 🔊 AUDIO

Dictation: Listen carefully to each word dictated to you and write it down below. Each word will be read twice.

٢-	_____	١-	_____
٤-	_____	٣-	_____
٦-	_____	٥-	_____
٨-	_____	٧-	_____
١٠-	_____	٩-	_____

D. The Letter *hā'* (ه) and Its Sound

The sound represented by this letter is pronounced like the *h* in the word "house." The difference between the English and Arabic *h* is that in English it is found mainly at the beginning of a syllable, whereas in Arabic it can be at the beginning or the end (e.g., English "hen"; Arabic هاب and تاةَ).

Examine how the different forms are written. The initial form is written with two loops, one within the other using only one stroke. Drawing the initial *hā'* might prove difficult at first, but one way to think about it is to simply draw an initial *dāl* and then form a loop where the lower tooth of the *dāl* is found. As for the medial shape, when handwritten the *hā'* *ʕ* is somewhat different from the printed shape ‎ـهـ. The final connected and independent forms of the *hā'* are similar to the *tā' marbūṭa* minus the dots.

Forms of the Two-Way Connector (ه)					
Symbol	**Name**	**Independent**	**Final connected**	**Medial**	**Initial**
h	*hā'*	ه	ـه	ـهـ	هـ

تمرين ١٩

Trace over the gray letters: The letters appear in their initial, medial, final, and independent positions:

ملاهٍ   تائِه   سَهْل   هِلال

تمرين ٢٠

Drawing letters: Write the following letters in their <u>initial</u>, <u>medial</u>, and <u>final</u> positions by writing the same letter in groups of three. Write as many groups as will fit on the line.

Example: بيب.

_____ ل

_____ ك

_____ م

_____ ه

تمرين ٢١ 🔊

Tracing: Listen to the following words as you read them and repeat each one during the pause. Then trace over the light-toned ones and copy them several times.

تَهافُت	تيه	شاه	مَهْدي	هادي
تَهافُت	تيه	شاه	مَهْدي	هادي
تَهافُت	تيه	شاه	مَهْدي	هادي

تمرين ٢٢

Forming words: See how many times you can write the same word on each line.

هادي _____

مَهدي _____

شاه _____

تيه _____

تهافُت _____

تمرين ٢٣

Spelling: Combine the letters in each set, including short vowels, to form words.

١- بَ + ه + ل + و + ل = _____

٢- مُ + ه + ا + تَ + ر + ا + ت = _____

٣- ا + ل + مَ + ل + ه + ا + ي = _____

٤- سَ + ف + ي + ه = _____

٥- فِ + د + ا + هُ = _____

٦- مَ + ه + ا + ر + ة = _____

٧- كَ + هْ + رَ + ب + ة = _____

٨- اِ + لْ + تِ + ه + ا + م = _____

٩- مَ + هْ + ن + ة = _____

١٠- أَ + جْ + هِ + ز + ة = _____

تمرين ٢٤ 🔊

Listen and recognize: Check the box next to the word you hear, as in the example.

رَفاة ☐	رَفاه ☑	:مِثال
حُسام ☐	هِشام ☐	١-
مَهروم ☐	مَحروم ☐	٢-
حَماس ☐	هامِس ☐	٣-
سُحام ☐	سِهام ☐	٤-
حَلال ☐	هِلال ☐	٥-
فَهْم ☐	فَحْم ☐	٦-
ساحِل ☐	ساهِل ☐	٧-
لَحْم ☐	لَهِم ☐	٨-
اِمْتِهان ☐	اِمْتِحان ☐	٩-
نَحْر ☐	نَهْر ☐	١٠-

تمرين ٢٥ 🔊

Dictation: Listen to each word dictated to you and write it down below. Each word is read twice.

_____ ٢-   _____ ١-

_____ ٤-   _____ ٣-

_____ ٦-   _____ ٥-

_____ ٨−   _____ ٧−

_____ ١٠−   _____ ٩−

تمرين ٢٦

Identify the letters: Identify the letters ل، ك، م، ه in different word positions in these excerpts from Arabic-language newspapers and in the zodiac signs below.

حَظُّكَ اليَوم

الأَسَد: لا تأْبَهْ بوِشايَةِ إنْسانٍ مُغْرِضٍ يَقْصِدُ بها الإساءةَ إلَيْك.	الحَمَل: الحياةُ مَليئةٌ بِمثل هذه المَواقِفِ فتَقَبَّلْ ذلِكَ بِصَدَرٍ رَحْب.

2. Objects from the Immediate Environment

جَريدَة   كِتاب   قَلَم   دَفْتَر

هاتِف   تِلْفاز   نَظّارَة   مِفْتاح

دَرّاجَة   مُسَجِّلَة   ساعة   حاسوب

سَيّارَة

تمرين ٢٧

Underline the word that does not belong in each set of words and explain your choice in English.

١- كِتاب   دَفْتَر   مُسَجِّلَة   جَريدَة

٢- نَظّارَة   دَرّاجَة   سَيّارَة

٣- تِلْفاز   مُسَجِّلَة   مِفْتاح   حاسوب

3. Expressing Possession

نَعَم، عِندي هاتِف. | عِندَكَ هاتِف؟

One way of expressing possession is by using a phrase made up of the adverbial عِنْدَ (literally, "at") and an attached pronoun. Together they form a compound word. In order to say to a man, "you have a book," you begin with the word عِنْدَ while attaching the pronoun كَ (you, m. sg.) suffixed to it, forming the construct عِنْدَكَ = "you have" (m. sg.). The word following عِنْدَكَ can be any noun, but in this case we used كِتاب to create "you have a book?" with rising intonation. Note that although the word عِنْدَكَ translates as "you have," it is **not** a verb in Arabic. Consider the following example:

١   عِنْدَ + كَ = عِنْدَكَ   *you (m. sg.) have*

٢   عِنْدَكَ + كِتاب = عِنْدَكَ كِتاب   *You have a book.*

- Since عِنْدَ takes the same possessive endings as most nouns, it might be helpful to think of a noun in English that is roughly equivalent, such as "possession." One would say "my possession," "your possession," "his possession," etc., in much the same manner as عِنْدَ is used in Arabic.

You are already familiar with another possessive suffix which you have used when introducing yourself, using "my name is . . ." (*ismī* اسمي). The final long vowel *yā'* (*ī* = ي) of this word is an attached pronoun, meaning "my." To say, "I have," use عِنْدَ plus the attached pronoun ي. The combination yields the word عِنْدي. Note that the *fatḥa* on the end of عِنْدَ is dropped when ي is suffixed, because two consecutive vowels are not permissible.

You can also express possession by attaching possessive pronouns to nouns. Let's take a couple of nouns that are listed on the previous page and add a *yā'* (*ī* = ي) at the end: كِتابي "my book," حاسوبي "my computer," هاتِفي "my phone," etc. You may use this formula (noun + ي) for any noun to attain "my _____."

4. Attached Pronouns

Every separate pronoun (e.g., أنا، أنتِ "I, you") has an attached counterpart that is suffixed to the end of nouns, prepositions, and verbs. When suffixed to nouns, they serve as possessive pronouns (e.g., ي، كَ "my, your"). When suffixed to verbs, they serve as direct objects (with a verb, ي requires a ن before it: ني). The table below titled **Separate and Attached Personal Pronouns** lists separate pronouns and their attached counterparts with examples of attached pronouns suffixed to nouns.

- Note that the third-person singular pronoun هُ (–hu = "his") is pronounced هِ (–hi) when preceded by either a *kasra* or the letter ي (e.g., فيهِ).

Separate and Attached Personal Pronouns				
	Meaning	**Example**	**Attached**	**Separate**
First Person	my (book)	كِتابي	ي	أنا
	our	كِتابُنا	نا	نَحْنُ
Second Person	your (m. sg.)	كِتابُكَ	كَ	أنْتَ
	your (f. sg.)	كِتابُكِ	كِ	أنْتِ
	your (m./f. dual)	كِتابُكُما	كُما	أنْتُما
	your (m. pl.)	كِتابُكُمْ	كُمْ	أنْتُم
	your (f. pl.)	كِتابُكُنَّ	كُنَّ	أنْتُنَّ
Third Person	his	كِتابُهُ	هُ	هُوَ
	her	كِتابُها	ها	هِيَ
	their (m./f. dual)	كِتابُهُما	هُما	هُما
	their (m. pl.)	كِتابُهُمْ	هُمْ	هُمْ
	their (f. pl.)	كِتابُهُنَّ	هُنَّ	هُنَّ

تمرين ٢٨

Find out from your neighbor: Find out who in class has the following:

a book   _____

a car   _____

a computer   _____

a watch   _____

a bike   _____

. . . and now report this information to your instructor.

Feminine Words and the Attached Pronoun

Almost all words that end with a *tā' marbūṭa* are feminine, which is why it is called the "feminine noun marker." The *tā' marbūṭa* itself does not make a sound unless it is in a possessive construct (e.g., *my* car, *his* car, *our* car, etc.). It is the *fatḥa* that always precedes the *tā' marbūṭa* that makes the characteristic *ah* sound at the end of most feminine words.

By attaching a pronoun to the *tā' marbūṭa*, we create the possessive construct previously mentioned. The name *tā' marbūṭa* means tied *tā'*, but when it comes into contact with the pronoun, it opens up, becoming the regular *tā'* ت that we learned in Unit 2. Examine the following:

sayyāratuka	سَيّارَة + كَ = سَيّارَتُكَ	٣
jarīdatī	جَريدَة + ي = جَريدَتي	٤

- Most of the time the *fatḥa* that precedes the *tā' marbūṭa* is not written because it is understood to be there, since it always precedes the *tā' marbūṭa*.

Attaching pronouns: Attach the pronoun to the noun and then give the meaning, as in the example.

his book	كِتابُهُ	مِثال: كِتاب + هُوَ =
_____ _____		١- ساعة + أنْتَ =
_____ _____		٢- دَفْتَر + نَحْنُ =
_____ _____		٣- نَظّارَة + هِيَ =
_____ _____		٤- حاسوب + أنا =
_____ _____		٥- دَرّاجَة + أنْتَ =
_____ _____		٦- ساعَة + أنا =
_____ _____		٧- جَريدَة + أنْتِ =
_____ _____		٨- سَيّارَة + هُوَ =
_____ _____		٩- كِتاب + نَحْنُ =
_____ _____		١٠- دَفْتَر + أنْتِ =

5. Describing National and Regional Affiliation

In this section we will learn how to take a noun and make it what we consider in English to be an adjective to describe our nationality (e.g., America > American; France > French, etc.). Describing one's national or regional affiliation involves providing information about one's place of origin or residence. This function requires the use of a noun called "noun of *nisba*" in Arabic. Read the following descriptions and try to figure out the nationalities of these two men.

أنا مِصريّ.

هُوَ مِصريّ.
هُوَ مِن مَدينةِ القاهِرة.

مارتِن لوثَر كِنغ أمريكيّ.
هُوَ مِن مَدينَةِ أتلانتا في وِلايَةِ جورجيا.

6. The Relative Noun *nisba* (اِسْمُ النِسبة)

The noun used to indicate affiliation is called a "relative noun." The Arabic word for it is *nisba* (literally "relation"). It is derived from a noun that refers to a city, country, region, ethnic group, etc. This process is fairly simple in Arabic. It involves adding one suffix to nouns. This suffix is made up of a doubled consonantal *yāʾ* يّ (–*iyy*). Here is how to make relative nouns:

- If we wish to derive a *nisba* from a noun that ends with a consonant, simply add a doubled (i.e., with a *šadda*—see Unit 6, section 3) consonantal *yāʾ* يّ (-*iyy*):

  Tunisian   تونِسيّ = يّ + تونِس   ←   تونِس   ٥

- If a noun ends with a *tāʾ marbūṭa* (ة) or *alif* (ا), drop them and add يّ:

  of Barza = Barzian   بَرْزيّ = يّ + بَرْز   ←   بَرْزَة   ٦

  French   فَرَنِسيّ = يّ + فَرَنْس   ←   فَرَنْسا   ٧

- If a noun ends with *yā'* and *tā' marbūṭa* (ية) or *yā'* and *alif* (يا), simply drop the *tā' marbūṭa* (ة) or *alif* (ا) and attach *yā'* (ي), which will make a doubled *yā'* with the original one:

Syrian	سوريّ	←	سورية ٨
Libyan	ليبيّ	←	ليبيا ٩

- If a noun has the definite article الـ "the" prefixed to it, drop it and attach the suffix يّ:

Sudanese سودان + يّ = سودانيّ	←	السودان ١٠

- Forming *nisba* nouns from some nouns having a long vowel requires dropping this long vowel (e.g., مدينة "city"):

civilian مَدن + يّ = مَدَنيّ	←	مَدينة ١١

- A small class of nouns, where an original letter (و) is deleted, requires the restoration of this letter before adding the suffix يّ:

paternal أبَ + و + يّ = أبَويّ	←	أب ١٢

- Some nouns end with *alif* and *hamza*, such as سَماء "sky." A relative noun may be formed by replacing the *hamza* with *wāw* (سَماويّ) or by keeping it (سَمائيّ).

7. Gender in Arabic Nouns

All Arabic nouns, even those denoting abstract notions, are either masculine or feminine. Many, but not all, feminine nouns are marked by a *tā' marbūṭa* (ة). If you wish to make a masculine *nisba* feminine, simply add a *tā' marbūṭa* to it.

Tunisian f. sg.	تونِسِيّة	= ة + *Tunisian m. sg.* تونِسيّ	١٣

- **Note**, however, that a few nouns that do not end in a *tā' marbūṭa* are feminine (e.g., أرض "floor, ground").

- The names of all cities and towns are feminine.

- Country names may be masculine or feminine.

تمرين ٣٠

Creating the _nisba_: Derive the masculine form of relative nouns (_nisba_) from the following nouns and then derive the feminine, as in the example.

Feminine	Masculine	Country	
لُبنانيّة	لُبنانيّ	لُبنان	مِثال:
		الهِنْد	١
		قطَر	٢
		السُّعودِيَّة	٣
		سورية	٤
		المَغْرِب	٥
		أمريكا	٦
		فَرَنسا	٧

تمرين ٣١

Fill in the blanks with the correct nationality:

مُحَمَّد سَلامة مِن مِصْرَ هُوَ (١) _____ . و«أوبرا ونفري» مِن أمريكا هِيَ
(٢) _____ . «روسَل كرو» من أستراليا هُوَ (٣) _____ ،
و«سيلين ديون» مِن كَنَدا هِيَ (٤) _____ . «فلادَمير بوتَن» من روسيا
هُوَ (٥) _____ .

تمرين ٣٢

Conversation: Hold a conversation in Arabic with a classmate, but this time add questions about your partner's nationality and possessions. To complete this task you must remember to (1) greet your classmate; (2) introduce yourself; (3) ask where he/she is from; (4) ask where that place is; (5) ask what nationality he/she is; (6) find out what he/she has/owns; and (7) say good-bye. Endeavor to meet as many of your classmates as you can and be creative with the language.

تمرين ٣٣

DVD: Watch Unit 5. While you are watching the dialogues, become an active participant by repeating what you hear, trying to imitate the sounds and inflections used in the scenes. Try to deduce the meaning of جِنْسِيّة through context and write your guess here:
_____.

Circle the best choice:

مِن أَيْنَ كرستين؟

ا- نيويورك

ب- بوسْطَن

ج- واشِنْطَن

د- بِتْسْبِرغ

SUMMARY

1. Possession may be expressed by using the adverb عِنْدَ plus one of the attached pronouns, e.g., عِنْدي كِتاب.

2. A relative noun (*nisba*) is derived by adding the suffix ّي to a noun, e.g., تونِسيّ تونِس.

3. Arabic nouns are either feminine or masculine. Many, but not all, feminine nouns have *tā' marbūṭa* (ة) as a suffix. A few masculine nouns end with *tā' marbūṭa* as well.

Unit 5   118

المُفْرَدات 🔊

Listen to the vocabulary items on the CD and practice their pronunciation.

you (m. pl.)	(pron., m., pl.) أَنْتُمْ
you (m./f. dual)	(pron., m./f., dual) أَنْتُما
you (f. pl.)	(pron., f., pl.) أَنْتُنَّ
television	(n., m.) تِلفاز ج تِلفازات
newspaper	(n., f.) جَريدَة ج جَرائِد
computer	(n., m.) حاسوب ج حَواسيب
bicycle	(n., f.) دَرّاجَة ج دَرّاجات
notebook	(n., m.) دَفتَر ج دَفاتِر
watch, clock	(n., f.) ساعَة ج ساعات
car	(n., f.) سَيّارَة ج سَيّارات
at	(adv.) عِندَ
(expresses possession with possessive pronouns)	
pen, pencil	(n., m.) قَلَم ج أقلام
book	(n., m.) كِتاب ج كُتُب
town, city	(n., f.) مَدينَة ج مُدُن
tape recorder	(n., f.) مُسَجِّلة ج مُسَجِّلات
key	(n., m.) مِفتاح ج مَفاتيح
we	(pron., pl.) نَحْنُ
relative adjective	(n., f.) نِسْبَة
eyeglasses	(n., f.) نَظّارة ج نَظّارات
telephone	(n., m.) هاتِف ج هَواتِف

they (m. pl.) . . . . (pron., m., pl.) هُمْ

they (m./f. dual) . . . . (pron., m./f., dual) هُما

they (f. pl.) . . . . (pron., f., pl.) هُنَّ

state . . . . (n., f.) وِلايَة ج وِلايات

وَ ما بِكُم مِن نِعمةٍ فَمِنَ الله

Decorative calligraphy of a Qur'anic phrase that reads
"Whatever blessings you have, come from God"

الوَحدَةُ السادِسةُ

Unit Six

Objectives

- Identifying classroom objects
- Introduction to the letters *alif maqṣūra* (ى) and *hamza* (ء)
- Introduction to the diacritical marks *šadda*, *madda*, *tanwīn*, and *sukūn*
- Introduction to the short *alif*
- Learning how foreign sounds are represented in Arabic script
- Learning more about phonological variation in colloquial Arabic

1. Familiar Objects in the Classroom

مِمْحاة	لَوْح	باب	نافِذَة
حَقيبَة	صورَة	كُرْسيّ	طاوِلَة
مِسْطَرَة	مِبْراة	مَكْتَب	حاسِبَة

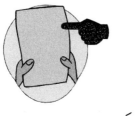

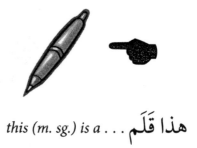

this (f. sg.) is a . . . هٰذِهِ وَرَقَة

this (m. sg.) is a . . . هٰذا قَلَم

تَمرين ١

Matching: Match words from the right-hand column with words in the left-hand column.
Take the time to practice writing Arabic by writing both words in the middle column.

نافِذَة		مِمْحاة	١
أمريكيّ		باب	٢
حَقيبة		كُرْسيّ	٣
مِبْراة		حاسوب	٤
حاسِبة		عَرَبيّ	٥
طاوِلَة			

تَمرين ٢

DVD: Watch Unit 6. While you are watching the dialogues, become an active participant by
repeating what you hear, trying to imitate the sounds and inflections used in the scenes.

1. Circle the words that John learned today:

قَلَم	نافِذة	مِمْحاة	لَوْح	باب	كُرْسيّ	صُورة	طاوِلة	أوْراق

2. Circle the things that John mentions he has with him:

قَلَم	أُوْراق	مِسْطَرة	طاوِلة	مِمْحاة	مِبْراة	صُورة

2. The Letters *alif maqṣūra* ى (*ā*) and *hamza* ء

A. The Letter *alif maqṣūra* ى (*ā*) and Its Sound

This letter is a variant of the regular *alif*. It is pronounced the same as *alif* (ى), but it is restricted to the final position in a word. It is written with one uninterrupted stroke, just like a *yā'* minus the two dots below it. Sometimes a tiny regular *alif* is written above it to distinguish it from *yā'* in regions where the two dots are not used below the final form of *yā'* (e.g., Egypt). If a suffix is attached to a word that ends in *alif maqṣūra*, it automatically changes to either a regular *alif* or to a medial *yā'*:

$$\text{فَتى} + \text{كِ} = \text{فَتاكِ}$$

$$\text{عَلى} + \text{كَ} = \text{عَلَيْكَ}$$

ــى	ى
Connected	**Independent**

تمرين ٣

Trace over the gray letters: This letter appears in its independent and connected positions:

جَرى   أُفْعى

Tracing: Listen to the following words as you read them and repeat each one during the pause. Then trace over the light-toned words below and copy them several times.

رَمى   موسى   هُدى   عَلى   سَلْوى   لَيْلى

رَمى   موسى   هُدى   عَلى   سَلْوى   لَيْلى

رَمى   موسى   هُدى   عَلى   سَلْوى   لَيْلى

تمرين ٥

Forming words: See how many times you can write the same word on each line.

لَيْلى _____

سَلْوى _____

عَلى _____

هُدى _____

موسى _____

رَمى _____

تمرين ٦

Spelling: Combine the letters in each set, including short vowels, to form words, as in the example:

مِثال: س + ا + ر + بْ + نِ   =   نِبْراس

١-   ى + ع + رَ   =   _____

٢-   ى + ر + تَ + شْ + يُ   =   _____

٣-   ى + ف + وَ   =   _____

٤-   ى + و + دْ + فَ   =   _____

تمرين ٧

Listen and recognize: Check the box next to the word you hear, as in the example.

عَلِيّ ☐		عَلى ☑	مِثال:
لاما ☐		لَمى ☐	١-
سُدى ☐		سودي ☐	٢-
رَمي ☐		رَمى ☐	٣-
لُبْنى ☐		لَبَنِيّ ☐	٤-
دَوِيّ ☐		دَوى ☐	٥-

تمرين ٨

Dictation: Listen to each word dictated to you and write it down below or on a ruled sheet of paper. Each word will be read twice.

_____ ٢-   _____ ١-

_____ ٤-   _____ ٣-

B. The Letter *hamza* (ء) and Its Sound

- The *hamza* can be placed above any one of the three long vowels, which serve *only* as seats for the *hamza* and have no phonetic value.

The basic form of *hamza* is illustrated below. It is disproportionately enlarged for you to see its shape. The *hamza* should be written in one uninterrupted stroke. It is written flush on the line in an independent position. Examine its relative size in the following word:

باء

The *hamza*		
Independent *hamza*	Make the tail after making its tooth	Start just like making an *'ayn*
ء		

In the initial position, if followed by a *fatḥa* or *ḍamma*, the *hamza* is written above an *alif*. If it is followed by a *kasra*, it is usually written below an *alif*. Remember that the *alif* has no phonetic value at all: it only serves as a seat for the *hamza*. When the *hamza* is followed by a *kasra*, it is usually placed below an *alif*, and there is no need to indicate the *kasra*.

$$ إ \qquad أُ \qquad أَ $$

The Letter *hamza* in the Initial Position

Writing the *hamza* above long vowels in medial and final positions follows a set of rules which will be covered gradually as you continue your study of Arabic. The *hamza* in the final position is written flush on the line if it is preceded by a long vowel (e.g., سوء، باء) or if it is preceded by a consonant with a *sukūn*, e.g., شَيْء، بَدْء. (The detailed rules for writing the *hamza* are covered in Lesson 24 of the *Ahlan wa Sahlan* textbook.)

تمرين ٩

Tracing: Listen to the following words as you read them and repeat each one during the pause. Then trace over the light-toned words below and copy them several times.

أُذَيْنَة	أَنْتِ	إزار	راء	إذا	رِفاء
أُذَيْنَة	أَنْتِ	إزار	راء	إذا	رِفاء
أُذَيْنَة	أَنْتِ	إزار	راء	إذا	رِفاءt

تمرين ١٠

Forming words: See how many times you can write the same word on each line.

رِفاء _____

إذا _____

راء _____

إزار _____

أنْتِ _____

أُذَيْنَة _____

تمرين ١١

Spelling: Combine the letters in each set, including short vowels, to form words.

١- ذ + ا + ت + سْ + أُ = _____

٢- ءَ + ا + ز + إِ = _____

٣- ك + و + ب + أَ = _____

٤- ء + ا + ي + رِ = _____

٥- لُ + أ + سْ + أُ = _____

The Sound of the *hamza*

The sound represented by the letter *hamza* is a consonant produced by stopping the breath momentarily in the glottis and then releasing it explosively—as when you lift something heavy. It is part of the English sound system, but it is not represented by a letter. For example, the words "above," "in," and "air" start with a glottal stop (i.e., *hamza*) which signals the release of the initial vowel in these words. One trick to producing the *hamza* in English is to take a word, "little" for instance, and then pronounce the word without the *t*'s, a naturally occurring phenomenon in Cockney English.

In Arabic, this sound can appear in any word position and is represented by the letter *hamza*, which incidentally occurs only in its independent form in the final word position.

Listen and recognize: Check the box next to the word you hear, as in the example.

☐	بَلى	☑	بَلاء	مِثال:	
☐	عَريض	☐	أُريد	١-	
☐	بَقاء	☐	نَقاء	٢-	
☐	نَشاء	☐	ثَناء	٣-	
☐	إذْن	☐	أذُن	٤-	
☐	أُبَيّ	☐	أبي	٥-	
☐	إناء	☐	أينَ	٦-	

3. Diacritical Marks

A. The *šadda* (ّ)

This mark indicates a doubled consonant. It is called *šadda* (شَدّة), meaning stress or emphasis. Doubling a consonant involves pronouncing it twice, such as the *k* in "book-keeping" and the *n* in "non-native." A *šadda* is placed above the doubled consonant. Examine the enlarged illustration.

The *šadda*	
The *šadda* above د	Make a backwards 'w' slightly canted
دّ	

- **Important note about the *šadda*:** The short vowel following a doubled consonant marked by a *šadda* is indicated above or below the *šadda*. The short vowels *fatḥa* and *ḍamma* are placed above the *šadda*, and the *kasra* below it, as in these examples:

$$الصَفِّ \quad الصَفُّ \quad الصَفَّ$$

Tracing: Listen to the following words as you read them and repeat each one during the pause. Then trace over the light-toned words below and copy them several times.

مُسَجِّلَة   نَظَّارَة   بَرَّاد   سَيَّارَة   بَسَّام   دَرَّاجَة

مُسَجِّلَة   نَظَّارَة   بَرَّاد   سَيَّارَة   بَسَّام   دَرَّاجَة

مُسَجِّلَة   نَظَّارَة   بَرَّاد   سَيَّارَة   بَسَّام   دَرَّاجَة

تمرين ١٤

Forming words: See how many times you can write the same word on each line.

دَرَّاجَة
_____

بَسَّام
_____

سَيَّارَة
_____

بَرَّاد
_____

نَظَّارَة
_____

مُسَجِّلَة
_____

تمرين ١٥

Spelling: Combine the letters in each set, including short vowels and other diacritical marks, to form words.

١- بَ + شْ + ش + ا + ر   =   _____

٢- حَ + دْ + د + ا + د   =   _____

٣- خَ + بْ + بَ + ا + ز   =   _____

٤- رَ + سْ + سَ + ا + م = _____

٥- شَ + دْ + دَ + ة = _____

٦- مِ + صْ + ر + يْ + يَ + ة = _____

٧- مَ + ا + دْ + دَ + ة = _____

تمرين ١٦

Listen and recognize: Check the box under "Doubled" if the word you hear contains a doubled consonant (i.e., with a *šadda*); check the box under "Not doubled" if the consonant is not doubled, as in the example.

	Doubled		Not doubled	
مِثال:	☐	بَراد	☑	بَرّاد
١-	☐		☐	
٢-	☐		☐	
٣-	☐		☐	
٤-	☐		☐	
٥-	☐		☐	
٦-	☐		☐	
٧-	☐		☐	
٨-	☐		☐	
٩-	☐		☐	
١٠-	☐		☐	

B. The *madda* (آ)

This mark is written above the letter *alif* to indicate a *hamza* followed by the long vowel *alif*. The mark *madda* (مَدّة) resembles a short, wavy line. The combination of sounds that results in a *madda* is illustrated below.

$$ آ = ا + ء $$

Tracing: Listen to the following words as you read them and repeat each one during the pause. Then trace over the light-toned words below and copy them several times.

شَآم	مَآثِر	قَرَآ	آلات	آداب
شَآم	مَآثِر	قَرَآ	آلات	آداب
شَآم	مَآثِر	قَرَآ	آلات	آداب

تمرين ١٨

Forming words: See how many times you can write the same word on each line.

آداب _____

آلات _____

قَرَآ _____

مآثِر _____

شَآم _____

تمرين ١٩

Spelling: Combine the letters in each set, including diacritics, to form words.

١- ء + ا + ر + ا + ء = _____

٢- م + رْ + ء + ا + ة = _____

٣- ء + ا + ل + ا + ف = _____

٤- ء + ا + فَ + ة = _____

٥- قُ + ء + ا + رْ + ن = _____

تمرين ٢٠

Listen and recognize: Check the box under "*Madda*" if the word read to you contains a *hamza* plus a long *alif*; check the box under "No *madda*" if a long *alif* only or a *hamza* only is pronounced, as in the example.

No *madda*		*Madda*		
☐	مادِر	☑	مآبِر	مِثال:
☐		☐		١-
☐		☐		٢-
☐		☐		٣-
☐		☐		٤-
☐		☐		٥-

C. The *tanwīn* (تَنْوين)

This is a phonological process that gives a *nūn*-like sound to three different endings, which are known as *tanwīn*. The first one is represented by a double *fatḥa* (˝), the second by a double *ḍamma* (˝), and the third by a double *kasra* (ˌ). They are pronounced –*an*, –*un*, –*in*, respectively.

Grammatically speaking, *tanwīn* indicates case and an indefinite status (e.g., "a man" as opposed to "the man"). It appears only on the last letter of a word; like short vowels, it is written above and below the letters it follows. A double *fatḥa* most often requires a silent *alif* as a seat (e.g., كتاباً), but if a word ends in a *hamza* preceded by a long *alif*, an *alif maqṣūra*, or a *tā' marbūṭa*, the double *fatḥa* may be placed above these three letters directly:

عَصاً مَساءً مَـلْهىً جريدةً

- **Note:** Words ending in a *hamza* but preceded by a consonant require an *alif* as a seat for *tanwīn* (e.g., بَدْءاً). A double *ḍamma* and a double *kasra* require no added seat. They are placed above and below the final letters, respectively:

جُزْءاً شَيْئاً كِتابٌ كِتابٍ

- **Note:** An *alif* is required for *tanwīn* after a *hamza*. In such a case, the *hamza* is written on the line and the *alif* stands independent if the letter preceding it (ز) is a one-way connector (جُزْءاً). The *hamza* is placed on a *yā'* if the preceding letter (ي) is a connector (شَيْئاً).

A double *ḍamma* may be written as two *ḍamma*s next to each other or as a diacritical mark that resembles a *ḍamma* with a little hook attached to it, as illustrated below.

$$\overset{\text{ٌ}}{د}$$

تمرين ٢١ 🔊

Tracing: Listen to the following words as you read them and repeat each one during the pause. Then trace over the light-toned words below and copy them several times.

أَهْلاً	سَيَّارَةً	مَساءً	حاسوبٍ	غُرْفَةٌ
أَهْلاً	سَيَّارَةً	مَساءً	حاسوبٍ	غُرْفَةٌ
أَهْلاً	سَيَّارَةً	مَساءً	حاسوبٍ	غُرْفَةٌ

تمرين ٢٢

Forming words: See how many times you can write the same word on each line.

أَهْلاً _____

سَيَّارَةً _____

مَساءً _____

حاسوبٍ _____

غُرْفَةٌ _____

تمرين ٢٣

Spelling: Combine the letters in each set, including diacritics, to form a word and then give its meaning in the second blank:

_____	_____	=	ن + ا + ف + ذ + ة + ٌ
_____	_____	=	حَ + ق + ي + ب + ة +
_____	_____	=	دَ + فْ + تَ + ر + ٌ
_____	_____	=	و + َ + ر + َ + ق + ة + ٌ
_____	_____	=	ه + ا + تِ + ف + ٍ
_____	_____	=	كِ + ت + ا + ب + ٌ
_____	_____	=	صـ + و + ر + َ + ة + ٌ

🔊 تمرين ٢٤

Listen and recognize: Listen to each word and mark the box under the appropriate *tanwin*:

	ٌ	ٍ	ً
-١	☐	☐	☐
-٢	☐	☐	☐
-٣	☐	☐	☐
-٤	☐	☐	☐
-٥	☐	☐	☐
-٦	☐	☐	☐

D. The *sukūn* سُكون (ْ)

This diacritical mark is represented by a tiny circle placed above a letter to indicate the absence of a vowel. No English equivalent to the *sukūn* exists, so what is its function? It shows that there is no syllable after the consonant or vowel it follows. If English used *sukūn*s, where would they occur in a word such as "class"? In fact, there would be two *sukūn*s—one between the *c* and *l*, and the other between the final two *s*'s. Why? Because there are no short vowels between those letters, and by extension these two consonant clusters cannot form a syllable.

The following words contain a sequence of two consonants, the first of which has a *sukūn* to indicate that there is no vowel to break the sequence of consonants.

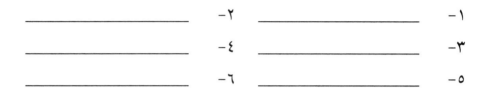

Dictation: Write down the words dictated to you and indicate all the short vowels and other diacritical marks, including the *sukūn*.

ــــــــــــــــــ	٢–	ــــــــــــــــــ	١–
ــــــــــــــــــ	٤–	ــــــــــــــــــ	٣–
ــــــــــــــــــ	٦–	ــــــــــــــــــ	٥–

4. The Short *alif*

There are a few words in Arabic that contain a regular long *alif* but are spelled without one. You may have wondered why the word هذا, for example, is pronounced هاذا, but spelled هذا, and why لكِنْ is thus spelled, but pronounced لاكِنْ. In fact, the long *alif* may be indicated by a special marker that resembles a tiny *alif* placed above the consonant it follows (indicated over the word الله below). This is referred to as the dagger *alif*. In practice, however, it is usually not written. Only in certain publications, such as the *Qur'ān* (the holy book of Muslims), can you find this diacritical mark. Since only a limited number of words exist that contain a long *alif* and are spelled without one, you will be able to recognize them even without the marker. Among these words are the following:

الله   لكِن   ذلِكَ   هؤُلاءِ   هذِه   هذا

Most of these words are already familiar to you. The third one (هؤُلاءِ) is a demonstrative pronoun like the first two, but it refers to human plurals. The fourth one (ذلِكَ) is also a demonstrative, but it refers to a distant masculine object. The short *alif* follows the first letter in all these words except الله, where it follows the second *lām*.

5. Representation of Foreign Sounds

There are a few sounds that exist in other languages but are not found in the Arabic sound system. Of these sounds, the following three are most commonly used because they are part of the sound systems of most European languages with which Arabic has close contact. Certain conventions in Arabic spelling address this deficiency.

Foreign Sound	Representation in Arabic
p	پ
v	ڤ
g	غ

The sound *g*, however, is represented by ج in Egypt because the letter ج is pronounced *g* in most parts of Egypt. It is represented by غ in the eastern part of the Arab world (the Levant) and in other regions where the ج is pronounced *j*. Some publications in the eastern part also use ج to represent *g*.

6. Colloquial Arabic: Phonological Variation

One difference between colloquial speech and Modern Standard Arabic exists at the phonological level. For example, the word قَلَم "pen" is pronounced *'alam* in most of Syria and urban areas in Egypt, while ظَريف "nice" is pronounced *ẓarīf*, نَظّارَة "eyeglasses" as *naddāra*, ذَهَب "gold" as *dahab*, لَذيذ "tasty" as *lazīz*, ثوم "garlic" as *tūm*, and ثانَويّ "secondary" as *sānawī*. As you can see, one sound may have up to two variants in colloquial speech in the Levantine area (i.e., Greater Syria). Note that these variants are not interchangeable. Below is a list of some sounds and their cognates in the colloquial Arabic spoken in the Levant.

Sound	Example	Standard	Colloquial
ق	قَلَم	*qalam*	*'alam* (urban)
	قَلَم	*qalam*	*galam* (rural)
ظ	نَظّارَة	*nazzāra*	*naddāra*

	ظَريف	*ẓarīf*	*ẓarīf*
ث	ثوم	*ṯūm*	*tūm*
	ثانَويّ	*ṯānawiyy*	*sānawī*
ذ	ذَهَب	*dahab*	*dahab*
	لَذيذ	*laḏīḏ*	*lazīz*

تمرين ٢٦

American cities and states in Arabic: Test your ability to identify at least ten American cities that appear on the map of the United States below and then write them down in Arabic. Use complete sentences as in the example provided below. This will allow you to apply the skills you have developed in using the Arabic script. Be sure to provide short vowels and other diacritical marks. Use the special conventions we learned in section 5 of this unit to represent non-Arabic sounds where necessary. Note that not all cities marked are state capitals.

Example: مَدينةُ شيكاغو في وِلايةِ إلينوي

- Can you guess what the word وِلاية means from context?

Letter identification: Identify the letter *hamza* (ء) in different word positions and the letter *alif maqṣūra* (ى) in this excerpt from the Arabic print media (a list of departures and arrivals).

حركة المطار

الطائرة السُعوديّة مِن الرياض ٥،٣٠

السُعوديّة إلى الرياض ٦،٣٠

الإيطاليّة إلى روما ٧،٣٠

السوريّة إلى إستنبول وموسكو ٧،٣٥

الألمانيّة إلى فرانكفورت ٧،٤٠

الطائرة السوريّة إلى دَير الزور والكُوَيْت ٨،٠٠

السوريّة إلى حَلَب وبرلين وكوبنهاغن ٨،٠٠

الطائرة اللبنانيّة مِن بَيْروت ٨،٣٠

السوريّة إلى حَلَب وباريس ٩،١٠

السوريّة إلى حَلَب وفرانكفورت ٩،١٠

اللبنانيّة إلى بَيْروت ٩،٢٠

الخليجيّة مِن أبو ظبي ١٠،١٠

الإمارات العربيّة مِن دُبَيّ ١٠،٣٠

الخليجيّة إلى أبو ظَبي ١٠،٤٥

الإمارات العربيّة إلى أبو ظَبي ١١،٢٠

Read and copy: Read and copy these examples of handwritten words:

محاريب ثعالب نيروز جيوش سلوى بيئة

مباراة نزيه فلك كريم لواء تنظير

■ **Cultural Note:**

A Traditional Family Room in a Small Arab Town or Village

Notice the kerosene lamp on the wall along with the electric lightbulb. A diesel oil space heater is used to heat and boil water in a kettle for tea. The cushions are placed against the walls where there is a wood floor. The floor is covered with wool rugs and carpets. People usually take their shoes off before stepping into the sitting area.

—Courtesy of the Arab Culture Notebook

المُفْرَدات 🔊

Listen to the vocabulary items on the CD and practice their pronunciation.

door . . . . (n., m.) باب ج أَبْواب

tanwīn . . . . (n., m.) تَنْوين
(diacritical mark, grammatical marker)

calculator . . . . (n., f.) حاسِبة ج حاسِبات

bag . . . . (n., f.) حَقّيبة ج حَقائِب

sukūn . . . . (n., m.) سُكون

šadda (diacritical mark that signifies . . . . (n., f.) شَدَّة
a doubled consonant)

picture . . . . (n., f.) صورة ج صُوَر

table . . . . (n., f.) طاوِلة ج طاوِلات

chair . . . . (n., m.) كُرسِيّ ج كَراسٍ

blackboard . . . . (n., m.) لَوْح ج ألواح

pencil sharpener . . . . (n., f.) مِبراة ج مَبارٍ/ مِبْرَيات

madda (a diacritical mark . . . . (n., f.) مَدّة ج مَدّات
that signifies a *hamza* followed by *alif*)

city, town . . . . (n., f.) مَدينة ج مُدُن

ruler . . . . (n., f.) مِسْطَرة ج مَساطِر

eraser . . . . (n., f.) مِمْحاة ج مَماحٍ/ مِمْحَيات

window . . . . (n., f.) نافِذة ج نَوافِذ

sheet of paper . . . . (n., f.) وَرَقة ج وَرَقات

state . . . . (n., f.) وِلاية ج وِلايات

Unit 6   140

Appendix A

Arabic Alphabet and Diacritical Marks

حروف الهجاء العربية
وعلامات التشكيل

الرمز Symbol	أشكال الحرف في مواضع الكلمة			اسم الحرف Name	الحرف Letter
	Final	**Medial**	**Initial**		
ā	ـا	ـا	ا	ألف	ا
b	ـب	ـبـ	بـ	باء	ب
t	ـت	ـتـ	تـ	تاء	ت
t̲	ـث	ـثـ	ثـ	ثاء	ث
j	ـج	ـجـ	جـ	جيم	ج
ḥ	ـح	ـحـ	حـ	حاء	ح
k̲	ـخ	ـخـ	خـ	خاء	خ
d	ـد	ـد	د	دال	د
d̲	ـذ	ـذ	ذ	ذال	ذ
r	ـر	ـر	ر	راء	ر
z	ـز	ـز	ز	زاي	ز
s	ـس	ـسـ	سـ	سين	س

š	شـ	ـشـ	شـ	شين	ش
ṣ	ـص	ـصـ	صـ	صاد	ص
ḍ	ـض	ـضـ	ضـ	ضاد	ض
ṭ	ـط	ـطـ	طـ	طاء	ط
ẓ	ـظ	ـظـ	ظـ	ظاء	ظ
ʿ	ـع	ـعـ	عـ	عين	ع
ġ	ـغ	ـغـ	غـ	غين	غ
f	ـف	ـفـ	فـ	فاء	ف
q	ـق	ـقـ	قـ	قاف	ق
k	ـك	ـكـ	كـ	كاف	ك
l	ـل	ـلـ	لـ	لام	ل
m	ـم	ـمـ	مـ	ميم	م
n	ـن	ـنـ	نـ	نون	ن
h	ـه	ـهـ	هـ	هاء	ه
w/ū	ـو	ـو	و	واو	و
y/ī	ـي	ـيـ	يـ	ياء	ي
ā	ـى			أَلِف مَقصورة	ى

t	ـة			تاء مربوطة	ة
ٔ	ـأـؤـئ	ـأـؤـئ	أإ	هَمزة	ء
a	fatḥa			فَتحة	َ
u	ḍamma			ضَمّة	ُ
i	kasra			كَسرة	ِ
-an	tanwīn			تَنوين بالفَتح	ً
-un	tanwīn			تَنوين بالضَمّ	ٌ
-in	tanwīn			تَنوين بالكَسر	ٍ
sukūn signifies the absence of a short vowel				سُكون	ْ
šadda indicates a doubled consonant				شَدّة	ّ
madda denotes a hamza followed by the long vowel alif				مَدّة	آ

143

Appendix B

A Key to the Arabic Sound System
and the Transliteration System Used in the Workbook

الحرف	الرمز	
Arabic Letter	**Roman Symbol**	**Example/Description**
ا	*ā*	*a* as in *far* and *bad*
ب	*b*	*b* as in *bet*
ت	*t*	*t* as in *two*
ث	*t̲*	*th* as in *three*
ج	*j*	*j* as in *judge*
ح	*ḥ*	*h*-like sound produced with constriction
خ	*k̲*	*ch* as in Scottish *loch* or German *Bach*
د	*d*	*d* as in *dip*
ذ	*d̲*	*th* as in *then*
ر	*r*	*r* as in Spanish *pero* (trilled *r*)
ز	*z*	*z* as in *zip*
س	*s*	*s* as in *sad*
ش	*š*	*sh* as in *show*
ص	*ṣ*	*s* as in *sod*
ض	*ḍ*	*d* as in *dark*
ط	*ṭ*	*t* as in *tar*

ظ	ẓ	*th* as in *thine*
ع	ʿ	a fricative sound produced in the throat
غ	ġ	roughly similar to the German *r*; a gargling sound
ف	f	*f* as in *fit*
ق	q	roughly similar to the *c* in *cot*, but further back
ك	k	*k* as in *kit*
ل	l	*l* as in *leak*
م	m	*m* as in *mint*
ن	n	*n* as in *nill*
ه	h	*h* as in *hat*
و	ū	*oo* as in *pool*
و	w	*w* as in *wet*
ي	ī	*ee* as in *feel*
ي	y	*y* as in *yet*
ى	ā	*a* as in *dad* (a form of *alif* in the final position)
ة	t	see the discussion on *tāʾmarbūṭa* in Unit 3 (Workbook)
ء	ʾ	glottal stop; the stop before *a* in *above*
ˎ	a	roughly similar to *u* as in *but*
ُ	u	*u* as in *pull*
ِ	i	*i* as in *bill*

145

Appendix C

Answer Key

The answer key provides answers to all the exercises in the *Letters and Sounds of the Arabic Language* workbook, including listening and comprehension exercises.

Unit One الوَحدةُ الأولى

Exercise 1:

Dialogue 1:	1. a. sāmir	b. nabīl	2. a. *tašarrafnā*
Dialogue 2:	1. a. kristīn	b. aḥmad	2. b. *as-salāmu ʿalaykum*

Exercise 13:

4– ذاد	3– راوا	2– زار	1– دارو
8– داذ	7– وادو	6– زارو	5– زود

Exercise 14:

Consonant – راواد –3	Vowel – دوذا –2	Vowel – زارو –1
Vowel – زادور –5		Consonant – واداد –4

Exercise 15:

4– رازو	3– ذور	2– زاد	1– واد
8– دود	7– داوود	6– زادور	5– راذاذ
		10– روزا	9– راد

Exercise 16:

dād–داد –2	*zād*–زاد –1
wād–واد –4	*rād*–راد –3
wāū–واو –6	*rādād*–راذاذ –5
wāzār–وازار –8	*dūd*–دود –7
dāūr–ذاور –10	*dūdāz*–ذوداز –9

Exercise 17:

1– درجات الحرارة العظمى والصغرى المتوقعة اليوم 18/23. زخات من المطر بعد الظهر.

2– اشرب كوكا كولا

3– الاقتصاد السوري بين «المطرقة» و«السندان» بقلم المحامي الأستاذ نذير سنان ص 5-7

146

Unit Two الوَحدَةُ الثانِيةُ

تمرين ٣

١- Self   ٢- Third person (m.)   ٣- Addressee (m.)   ٤- Third person (f.)

٥- Addressee (f.)   ٦- Addressee (m.)

تمرين ٤

Dialogue 1:   1. d. aḥmad   2. b. 'afwan
Dialogue 2:   1. a. ranā   b. manāl   2. b. šukran

تمرين ١٣

١- نُريد	٢- زُبَيْدي	٣- رَتيب	٤- يابان
٥- بُدور	٦- ثابِت	٧- بَوادِر	٨- نَبات
٩- وَزير	١٠- نادِر	١١- تُراث	١٢- رَذاذ
١٣- وادي	١٤- باتوا		

تمرين ١٥

١- دَب short	٢- زور long	٣- ديب long	٤- بُن short
٥- يار long	٦- يوب long	٧- دار long	٨- بَرْد short

تمرين ١٦

١- داني	٢- بارود	٣- روبي	٤- داري
٥- ثُبور	٦- نادِر	٧- بَريد	٨- رَباب

تمرين ١٧

١- رَبيب	٢- ثابِت	٣- نوري	٤- باري
٥- نابي	٦- بوران	٧- رَذاذ	٨- دُب
٩- بَرود	١٠- بَوادِر	١١- وَزير	١٢- داوود
١٣- وَتير	١٤- رَتيب		

تمرين ١٨

جونية بيروت بعبدا **بيت الدين** سوريا راشيا صيدا مرجعيو**ن** صور **بنت** جبيل فلسطين

عملية السلام **تتعثر** في واشنطن لكن الأمريكيين متفائلو**ن** بالنتائج

قام وزير الدولة الإيراني بزيارة **ثانية** إلى تونس في هذا الشهر.

147

الوَحدَةُ الثالِثةُ Unit Three

تمرين ١

Dialogue 1:   1. c. thank God, well   2. c. not bad
Dialogue 2:   c. *mā akhbāruki*
Dialogue 3:   b. *ta'bān*

تمرين ٧

٤- شَراشيب	٣- سَيارين	٢- شَريد	١- تِشرين
٨- شَوارِب	٧- سَراب	٦- يابوس	٥- تَشويش
	١١- يَسار	١٠- شَباب	٩- يُشير

تمرين ٨

٤- راش	٣- روسيّ	٢- شَراب	١- تَسديد
٨- سودان	٧- يَسار	٦- ناشِز	٥- شَنَب
	١٠- سار	٩- شِرْيان	

تمرين ٩

٤- ديدان	٣- شين	٢- سَردين	١- داسو
٨- ياسين	٧- ناشِز	٦- رَشاش	٥- شادور
	١٠- سَبَب	٩- شَراشيب	

تمرين ١٤

٤- خَسيس	٣- شَخير	٢- سِنْجاب	١- رِحاب
٨- سَحاب	٧- ساخِرون	٦- جوري	٥- رَبيح
	١٠- اِنْحِدار	٩- جيران	

تمرين ١٥

٤- جَرَش	٣- حَديث	٢- حَرير	١- خَراب
٨- شَخير	٧- روح	٦- تَحْذير	٥- حَديد
	١٠- ساحِر	٩- خاسِر	

تمرين ١٦

٤- حَبيبي	٣- خَروف	٢- جَبان	١- حَراج
٨- تَحْذير	٧- حَرير	٦- خاسِر	٥- حَشيش
	١٠- خَراب	٩- شَخير	

تمرين ٢٠

٤- ثاقِب	٣- فُنون	٢- تَقارير	١- رَقيب
٨- سارِق	٧- شَفيق	٦- نُقود	٥- فُرات
١٢- فِرْدَوْس	١١- قِرْش	١٠- شُروق	٩- قَريب

تمرين ٢١

٤- أفْراح	٣- فَنادِق	٢- ثُقْب	١- سَحيق
٨- اِحْتِراق	٧- فَراديس	٦- فُسْتُق	٥- رِفاق
		١٠- شُروخ	٩- سَقَر

تمرين ٢٥

٤- شَريفَة	٣- دفينة	٢- جَريدتي	١- خَشْيَتي
٨- حَقيبَتي	٧- زيارَتي	٦- قارورَتي	٥- حارِسَة
		١٠- سَفينَتي	٩- فَخْرَة

تمرين ٢٦

٤- سفينتي	٣- حياتي	٢- سُفرة	١- فَريدة
		٦- حقيبتي	٥- خسارة

تمرين ٢٧

خَبَر

سَتَبْدَأُ غَداً الأحَدَ أعْمالُ الدَورةِ التَدْريبِيَّةِ لِلإعلامِ الزِراعيِّ والّتي تُقامُ بِرعايَةِ السّيّدِ خَليل عَرنوق وَزير الزِراعة.

حَرَكَةُ القِطارات

مِن دِمَشْق مُباشَرةً دونَ تَوَقُّفٍ إلى حَلَب ١٦،١٠ مِن دِمَشْق إلى حِمْص، حَماة، حَلَب الرَقَّة دَيْر الزَوْر الحَسَكَة القامِشلي ١٧،٢٥ إلى طَرطوس وَاللاذِقِيَّة ١٣١، •

قريش قريباً جداً

هل لديك ما يلزم لتصنع التاريخ

لعبة استراتيجية عربية

فهل تملك ما يلزم لتقود الأمة وتصنع التاريخ!

الوَحدَةُ الرابِعَةُ Unit Four

تمرين ١

Dialogue 1: 1. b. Damascus   2. a. New York
Dialogue 2: 1. d. Fez   2. a. dānya

تمرين ٨

٤- صُدور	٣- ضَفيرة	٢- فُرَص	١- صَرير
٨- قَوانِص	٧- رَصين	٦- قَوارِض	٥- يَصْفِرُ
١٢- صَفَّارَة	١١- رَصيف	١٠- اِنْخِفاض	٩- حاضِر
	١٥- أبْيَض	١٤- اِخْتِصاص	١٣- قُضْبان

تمرين ٩

٤- رُدود	٣- ضَجيج	٢- رَصين	١- فَصيحة
٨- ضاري	٧- رَصيف	٦- ساد	٥- فَريدة
		١٠- يَصْرِف	٩- ساري

تمرين ١٠

٤- وَصفة	٣- ضَروري	٢- صَفيح	١- صَرصور
٨- رَصيب	٧- ضَرير	٦- حَصير	٥- صَرير
		١٠- صُدور	٩- ضَفيرة

تمرين ١٥

٤- رُطَب	٣- فَظاظة	٢- قِطار	١- طَرْبوش
٨- بَساطة	٧- ظَريف	٦- طَريق	٥- بوص
		١٠- تَشْطيب	٩- خَريطة

تمرين ١٦

٤- طارِق	٣- ظافِر	٢- ظَريف	١- رَتيب
٨- بَتَر	٧- أطراب	٦- ظَرْف	٥- تين
		١٠- حَظَر	٩- نَذير

تمرين ١٧

٤- شَوط	٣- طَريف	٢- ظَبية	١- طَيْش
٨- طَربوش	٧- شَظايا	٦- شُباط	٥- فَظاظة
		١٠- حَظيرة	٩- قِطار

تمرين ١٨

| ٣- قار – car | ٢- داد – dad | ١- فاظَر – father |

٥- سيصا – seesaw	٤- تانْجَرين – tangerine
٨- داينْجَر – danger	٦- ضائَر – daughter ٧- شائَر – shatter

تمرين ٢٣

٤- بَديع	٣- دَعْد	٢- شُغور	١- عِفْريت
٨- اِسْتَطاع	٧- تَفْريغ	٦- فَظيع	٥- تُبوغ
		١٠- صِباغ	٩- غَريب

تمرين ٢٤

٤- صَبَغَ	٣- يُذيع	٢- يَعرِف	١- غَدير
٨- عَرَب	٧- فَرَغَ	٦- تَغيض	٥- غَريق
		١٠- غُراب	٩- تَبْغ

تمرين ٢٥

٤- سَريع	٣- رَديد	٢- ظَرْبان	١- صَديد
٨- فصيح	٧- تاب	٦- عُضو	٥- صَبَرَ

تمرين ٢٦

Boise –٤	Utah –٣	Syria –٢	Beirut –١
Baghdad –٨	Baton Rouge –٧	Tunisia –٦	Arizona –٥
		Wichita –١٠	Indiana –٩

تمرين ٢٩

١- تنطلق الأحد وتجمع حقائب مدرسية وتبرعات عينية
«بصمة عطاء» من مدارس الدولة لطلاب لبنان

٢- «وطني» ينظم دورة متخصصة حول تغيير الذات في دلما

٣- خلال مفاجآت صيف دبي
برنامج وطني ينظم ندوات اجتماعية وتربوية وصحية

٤- ١٠٠ طفل لبناني يطالبون أنان
بالتدخل لوقف العدوان

دبي – الإمارات اليوم: وقّع مئة طفل لبناني مقيمين في الدولة، بطاقة موجهة إلى
الأمين العام للأمم المتحدة كوفي أنان يطلبون منه فيها التدخل الفوري لوقف
الحرب في لبنان. وقالت آية صادق (١٠ أعوام) إن شعورا بالحزن الشديد ينتابها
وهي تشاهد الأطفال والأبرياء يسقطون نتيجة هذه الحرب التي تشنها إسرائيل.
وتحول لبنان. . البلد الجميل إلى دمار واسع.
وركز الأطفال في البطاقة على حق اقرانهم في لبنان في العيش بأمان، وفي أن
يلهوا ويستمتعوا بحياتهم، بدلا من أن يكونوا أهدافا للقتل.

الوَحدَةُ الخامِسةُ Unit Five

٤- الإسلام   ٣- عَسَل   ٢- بُلْبُل   ١- اللَيَالي

٨- طالِبة   ٧- نَوال   ٦- صَليب   ٥- جَلال

              ١١- إغلاق   ١٠- تَقْليد   ٩- تِلْفاز

تمرين ٥

٤- لادِن   ٣- بُلْبُل   ٢- والي   ١- بِلال

٨- لازِق   ٧- وَلَدي   ٦- بَلَدي   ٥- لَبيب

تمرين ٦

٤- دال   ٣- رِسالة   ٢- خَليل   ١- لَسْنا

                          ٦- لَذيذ   ٥- بَلَل

تمرين ١٠

٤- بُرْكان   ٣- شُكوك   ٢- كُسوف   ١- كُرْدوس

٨- تَكْرير   ٧- كَواكِب   ٦- كَبْكَب   ٥- إحْتِكاك

              ١٠- كَبير   ٩- تَشْكيل

تمرين ١١

٤- فُكوك   ٣- فَريق   ٢- شاكِر   ١- كُوَيت

٨- رَقيق   ٧- دَلَك   ٦- كَسَب   ٥- قاسي

              ١٠- كَلْب   ٩- شُكوك

تمرين ١٢

٤- كُفوف   ٣- صُكوك   ٢- كان   ١- كَليلة

٨- كِبريت   ٧- سُلوك   ٦- شاك   ٥- كاري

              ١٠- رُكّاب   ٩- كَواكِب

تمرين ١٦

٤- مُقيم   ٣- كِرام   ٢- مُسْلِمون   ١- بَلْسَم

٨- مَجموعة   ٧- مَشْمول   ٦- المُدير   ٥- مُشْمِس

              ١٠- مُمْتاز   ٩- ميلادي

تمرين ١٧

٤- صَميم   ٣- دَمَس   ٢- مَسار   ١- مُدير

٨- ذِمَم   ٧- سَلام   ٦- لامِس   ٥- مُراد

تمرين ١٨

٤- مِرحاض	٣- أُمَم	٢- سُموم	١- مَلايين
٨- جامِعة	٧- تَمام	٦- تَمرين	٥- صَميم
		١٠- قَلَم	٩- قُمامة

تمرين ٢٣

٤- سَفيه	٣- المَلاهي	٢- مُهاتَرات	١- بَهلول
٨- اِتِّهام	٧- كَهرَبة	٦- مَهارة	٥- فِداهُ
		١٠- أُجْهِزة	٩- مِهْنة

تمرين ٢٤

٤- سِهام	٣- حَماس	٢- مَحروم	١- هِشام
٨- لَخْم	٧- ساجِل	٦- فَهْم	٥- هِلال
		١٠- نَهر	٩- اِمْتِحان

تمرين ٢٥

٤- هامِش	٣- تَيْه	٢- مَهزوم	١- هارون
٨- هِلال	٧- سَهَل	٦- هِمَم	٥- تاه
		١٠- جِهاز	٩- فَهِم

تمرين ٢٦

اليَوم

الحَمَل: الحياةُ مَليئةٌ بِمِثل هذه المَواقِفِ فَتَقَبَّل ذلِكَ بِصَدرٍ رَحْب.

الأسَد: لَا تَأْبَهْ بِوِشايةِ إنسانٍ مُغْرِضٍ يَقْصِدُ بها الإساءةَ إلَيْك.

القوس الجدي الدلو الحوت الحمل الثور الجوزاء السرطان الأسد العذراء الميزان العقرب

تمرين ٢٧

١- مُسَجِّلَة – the other words are related to reading

٢- نَظَّارَة – the other words deal with transportation

٣- مِفتاح – the other words are masculine

تمرين ٢٩

٢- دَفتَرُنا – our notebook		١- ساعتُكَ – your (m. sg.) watch
٤- حاسوبي – my computer		٣- نَظّارَتُها – her glasses
٦- ساعَتي – my watch		٥- دَرّاجَتُكَ – your (m. sg.) bike
٨- سَيّارتُه – his car		٧- جَريدَتُكِ – your (f. sg.) newpaper
١٠- دَفتَرُكِ – your (f. sg.) notebook		٩- كِتابُنا – our book

153

تمرين ٣٠

١- هِنْديّ – هِنْديّة   ٢- قَطَريّ – قَطَريّة   ٣- سُعوديّ – سُعوديّة   ٤- سوريّ – سوريّة

٥- مَغْرِبيّ – مَغْرِبيّة   ٦- أمريكيّ – أمريكيّة   ٧- فَرَنسيّ – فَرَنسيّة

تمرين ٣٠

١- مِصْريّ   ٢- أمريكيّة   ٣- أوسْتَراليّ   ٤- كَنَديّة

٥- روسيّ

تمرين ٣٣

(ج) واشِنْطَن

الوَحدةُ الخامِسةُ Unit Six

تمرين ١

١- مِمْحاة – مِبْراة   ٢- باب – نافِذة   ٣- كُرْسيّ – طاوِلة

٤- حاسوب – حاسِبة   ٥- عَرَبيّ – أمريكيّ

تمرين ٢

١- طاوِلة، صورة، كُرْسيّ، باب، لَوْح، نافِذة، قَلَم

٢- مِبْراة، مِمْحاة، مِسْطَرة، أوْراق، قَلَم

تمرين ٦

١- رَعى   ٢- يُشْتَرى   ٣- وَفى   ٤- فَدْوى

تمرين ٧

١- لاما   ٢- سُدى   ٣- رَمى   ٤- لُبْنى

٥- دَوى

تمرين ٨

١- هَمى   ٢- ذُرى   ٣- سُدى   ٤- هُدى

تمرين ١١

١- أُستاذ   ٢- إزاءَ   ٣- أبوك   ٤- رِياء

٥- أسْألُ

تمرين ١٢

١- أُريد   ٢- بَقاء   ٣- نَشاء   ٤- أُذُن

٥- أبي   ٦- إناء

154

تمرين ١٥

٤- رَسَّام	٣- خَبَّاز	٢- حَدَّاد	١- بَشَّار
	٧- مادَّة	٦- مِصْرِيَّة	٥- شَدَّة

تمرين ١٦

٢- ثَمان – not doubled	١- شُبَّاك – doubled
٤- ساحِر – not doubled	٣- سَحّار – doubled
٦- مَرّة – doubled	٥- هَجّان – doubled
٨- مادّة – doubled	٧- طاوِلة – not doubled
١٠- نافِذة – not doubled	٩- أمريكيّ – doubled

تمرين ١٩

٤- آفة	٣- آلاف	٢- مِرْآة	١- آراء
			٥- قُرآن

تمرين ٢٠

٤- آثار – *madda*	٣- مِرآب – *madda*	٢- مَأرِب – no *madda*	١- أثَر – no *madda*
			٥- أدَب – no *madda*

تمرين ٢٣

٢- حَقيبةٍ – a bookbag	١- نافِذةً – a window
٤- وَرَقةً – a piece of paper	٣- دَفتَرٌ – a notebook
٦- كِتابٌ – a book	٥- هاتِفٍ – a telephone
	٧- صورَةً – a picture

تمرين ٢٤

٤- مساءً	٣- أهلٌ	٢- بيتٍ	١- عفواً
	٦- جيمٍ		٥- دينٌ

تمرين ٢٥

٤- سِنْجاب	٣- غُرْفة	٢- مِلْح	١- بَحْر
	٦- تَفْكير		٥- مِصْر

تمرين ٢٧

المطار

الطائرة السُعوديّة مِن الرياض ٥،٣٠

السُعوديّة إلى الرياض ٦،٣٠

الإيطاليّة إلى روما ٧،٣٠

السوريّة إلى إستنبول وموسكو ٧،٣٥

الأَلمانيّة إلى فرانكفورت ٧،٤٠

الطائرة السوريّة إلى دَير الزور والكُوَيْت ٨،٠٠

السوريّة إلى حَلَب وبرلين وكوبنهاغن ٨،٠٠

الطائرة اللبنانيّة مِن بَيْروت ٨،٣٠

السوريّة إلى حَلَب وباريس ٩،١٠

السوريّة إلى حَلَب وفرانكفورت ٩،١٠

اللبنانيّة إلى بَيْروت ٩،٢٠

الخليجيّة مِن أبو ظبي ١٠،١٠

الإمارات العربيّة مِن دُبَيّ ١٠،٣٠

الخليجيّة إلى أبو ظَبي ١٠،٤٥

الإمارات العربيّة إلى أبو ظَبي ١١،٢٠

Appendix D

DVD Scripts

أهلا وسهلا
حروف اللغة العربية وأصواتها

سـيناريو وحوار
ديما بركات

إشراف ومتابعة لغوية
د. مهدي العش
ديما بركات
آلن كلارك

الوحدة الأولى

الحوار الأول:

– مرحبا.

– أهلاً وسهلاً.

– أنا اسمي سامر.

– وأنا نبيل.

– تشرفنا نبيل.

– وأنا أيضاً.

الحوار الثاني:

– السلام عليكم.

– وعليكم السلام.

– أنا كرستين.

– وأنا أحمد.

– فرصة سعيدة أحمد.

– وأنا أيضاً.

استمعوا وكرروا:

أهلاً وسهلاً	مرحباً
وعليكم السلام	السلام عليكم
مساء النور	مساء الخير
صباح النور	صباح الخير
الله يسلمك	مع السلامة

الوحدة الثانية

الحوار الأول:

- مساء الخير.

- مساء النور.

- عفواً، هل أنت سامي.

- لا، أنا لست سامي، أنا أحمد.

- أنا آسف.

- لا مشكلة.

الحوار الثاني:

- مرحباً.

- أهلاً وسهلاً.

- هل أنتِ منال؟

- نعم، أنا منال.

- أنا رنا رفيقة هالة.

- أهلاً وسهلاً رنا، تشرفنا.

- شكراً

الوحدة الثالثة

الحوار الأول:

- صباح الخير.

- صباح النور.

- كيف حالك؟

- الحمد لله بخير وأنتِ؟

- لا بأس.

الحوار الثاني:

- مرحباً.

- أهلاً وسهلاً.

- وما أخبارك؟

- أخباري جيدة والحمد لله.

الحوار الثالث:

- مرحباً.

- أهلاً وسهلاً.

- كيف حالك؟

- تعبان قليلاً.

- سلامتك.

- الله يسلمك.

اسمعوا وكرروا:

	كيف حالك؟
تمام.	
بخير والحمد لله.	
جيد	
لا بأس	
تعبان.	

الوحدة الرابعة

الحوار الأول:

- السلام عليكم.

- وعليكم السلام.

- أنا نبيل من الشام وأنت؟

- وأنا جون من أمريكا، من ولاية نيويورك. أين الشام؟

- الشام هي عاصمة سورية.

- تشرفنا.

- تشرفنا.

الحوار الثاني:

- مرحباً.

- أهلاً وسهلاً.

- أنا اسمي رشا، أنا من المغرب، من مدينة فاس.

- وأنا اسمي دانية، أنا من مصر، من مدينة الإسكندرية.

- فرصة سعيدة.

- وأنا أيضاً.

الوحدة الخامسة

الحوار الأول:

- صباح الخير .

- صباح النور .

- ما اسمك؟

- اسمي كريستين .

- من أين أنت؟

- أنا من واشنطن .

- ما جنسيتك؟

- جنسيتي أمريكية.

- تشرفنا.

- وأنا أيضاً.

أنا من عمان، أنا أردنية، جنسيتي أردنية.	أنا من حمص، أنا سوريّ، جنسيتي سوريّة.
أنا من بيروت، أنا لبنانية، جنسيتي لبنانية.	أنا من القاهرة، أنا مصريّ، جنسيتي مصرية.
أنا من لندن، أنا بريطاني، جنسيتي بريطانية.	أنا من دبي، أنا إماراتي، جنسيتي إماراتية.
أنا من باريس، أنا فرنسيّة، جنسيتي فرنسية.	أنا من أتلانتا، أنا أمريكي، جنسيتي أمريكية.

الوحدة السادسة

الحوار الأول:

- مرحباً أيمن.

- أهلاً وسهلاً جون، كيف حالك؟

- أنا بخير والحمد لله.

- ماذا تعلمت في الجامعة اليوم.

- تعلمت أسماء الأشياء الموجودة في الصف.

- ما هي؟

- لوح، كرسي، قلم، باب، نافذة، طاولة، وصورة.

- وما هذه الأشياء التي معك؟

- هذه ممحاة، وهذا قلم، وهذه مبراة، وهذه مسطرة، وهذه أوراق.

- ممتاز، أنت تعلمت أسماء كل هذه الأشياء.

- نعم وأنا سعيد جداً.

- وأنا أيضاً.

Cumulative Vocabulary
أ

Abu Dhabi [4] . . . . (n., f.) أبو ظَبي

proper noun (man's name) [1] . . . . (n., m.) أديب

Jordan [4] . . . . (n., m.) الأردُن

Arizona [4] . . . . (n., f.) أريزونا

name [1] . . . . (n., m.) إسم ج أسماء

good-bye [1] . . . . إلى اللِقاء

name of the letter *alif* [1] . . . . (n., f.) أَلِف

may God keep you safe [1] . . . . الله يُسَلِّمُك

United Arab Emirates [4] . . . . (n., f.) الإمارات

I [1] . . . . (pron.) أنا

you (m. sg.) [2] . . . . (pron., m.) أَنْتَ

you (f. sg.) [2] . . . . (pron., f.) أَنْتِ

you (m. pl.) [5] . . . . (pron., m., pl.) أنتُم

you (m./f. dual) [5] . . . . . . (pron., m/f, dual) أنتُما

you (f. pl.) [5] . . . . (pron., f., pl.) أنتُنَّ

Indiana [4] . . . . (n., f.) إنديانا

hello, welcome (response to a greeting) [1] . . . . أهلاً

also [1] . . . . أيضاً

proper noun (man's name) [2] . . . . (n., m.) أيمَن

where (question particle) [4] . . . . أينَ

ب

name of the letter *bā'* [2] . . . . (n., f.) باء

door [6] . . . . (n., m.) باب ج أبْواب

Baton Rouge [4] . . . . (n., f.) باتِن روج

Bahrain [4] . . . . (n., f.) البَحرَين

fine, well [3] . . . . بِخَيْر

Baghdad (capital of Iraq) [4] . . . . (n., f.) بَغْداد

Boise [4] . . . . (n., f.) بويزي

Beirut (capital of Lebanon) [4] . . . . (n., f.) بَيْروت

ت

name of the letter *tā'* [2] . . . . (n., f.) تاء

pleased to meet you (literally: *we've been honored*) [1] . . . . تَشَرَّفْنا

tired [3] . . . . تَعْبان

perfect; great [3] . . . . تَمام

television [5] . . . . (n., m.) تِلفاز ج تِلفازات

tanwīn (diacritical mark, grammatical marker) [6] . . . . (n., m.) تَنْوين

Tunis, Tunisia [4] . . . . (n., f.) تونِس

ث

name of the letter *ṯā'* [2] . . . . (n., f.) ثاء

ج

newspaper [5] . . . . (n., f.) جَريدَة ج جَرائِد

Algiers, Algeria [4] . . . . (n., f.) الجَزائِر

Djibouti [4] . . . . (n., f.) جيبوتي

good [3] . . . . جَيِّد

name of the letter *jīm* [3] . . . . (n., f.) جيم

ح

name of the letter *ḥā'* [3] . . . . (n., f.) حاء

computer [5] . . . . (n., m.) حَواسيب ج حاسوب

calculator [6] . . . . (n., f.) حاسِبات ج حاسِبة

condition, circumstance [3] . . . . (n., f.) أحْوال ج حال

bag [6] . . . . (n., f.) حَقائِب ج حَقيبة

Thank God, praise be to God [3] . . . . الحَمدُ لِلّه

خ

name of the letter *ḵā'* [3] . . . . (n., f.) خاء

news [3] . . . . أخْبار ج خَبَر

Khartoum (capital of the Sudan) [4] . . . . (n., f.) الخُرطوم

د

name of the letter *dāl* [1] . . . . (n., f.) دال

bicycle [5] . . . . (n., f.) دَرّاجات ج دَرّاجَة

notebook [5] . . . . (n., m.) دَفاتِر ج دَفتَر

Damascus (capital of Syria) [4] . . . . (n., f.) دِمَشْق

Doha (capital of Qatar) [4] . . . . (n., f.) الدَوحة

ذ

name of the letter *ḏāl* [1] . . . . (n., f.) ذال

ر

name of the letter *rā'* [1] . . . . (n., f.) راء

Rabat (capital of Morocco) [4] . . . . (n., f.) الرِباط

proper noun (woman's name) [2] . . . . (n., f.) رَنا

Riyadh (capital of Saudi Arabia) [4] . . . . (n., f.) الرِياض

ز

name of the letter *zāy* [1] . . . . (n., f.) زاي

س

watch, clock [5] . . . . (n., f.) ساعَة ج ساعات

proper noun (man's name) [2] . . . . (n., m.) سامي

sukūn [6] . . . . (n., m.) سُكون

Saudi Arabia [4] . . . . (n., f.) السُعودية

peace be upon you (greeting) [1] . . . . السَلامُ عَلَيْكُمْ

the Sudan [4] . . . . (n., m.) السودان

Syria [4] . . . . (n., f.) سورِيَة

car [5] . . . . (n., f.) سَيّارَة ج سَيّارات

name of the letter *sīn* [3] . . . . (n., f.) سين

ش

another name for Damascus; historically Greater Syria [4] . . . . (n., m.) الشام

šadda (diacritical mark that signifies a doubled consonant) [6] . . . . (n., f.) شَدَّة

thank you [2] . . . . شُكْراً

name of the letter *šīn* [3] . . . . (n., f.) شين

ص

name of the letter *ṣād* [4] . . . . (n., f.) صاد

good morning [3] . . . . صَباحُ الخَيْر

good morning (response = *ṣabāḥu n-nūr*) [3] . . . . صَباحُ النور

Sanaa (capital of Yemen) [4] . . . . (n., f.) صَنْعاء

picture [6] . . . . (n., f.) صورة ج صُوَر

Somalia [4] . . . . (n., m.) الصومال

ض

name of the letter *ḍād* [4] . . . . (n., f.) ضاد

ط

table [6] . . . . (n., f.) طاوِلة ج طاوِلات

name of the letter *ṭā'* [4] . . . . (n., f.) طاء

Tripoli (capital of Libya) [4] . . . . (n., f.) طَرابُلُس الغَرب

ظ

name of the letter *ẓā'* [4] . . . . (n., f.) ظاء

ع

capital [4] . . . . (n., f.) عاصِمة ج عواصِم

Iraq [4] . . . . (n., m.) العِراق

Arab [4] . . . . (n., m.) عَرَبيّ ج عَرَب

excuse me; pardon; you're welcome (as a response to شُكْراً) [2] . . . . عَفْواً

Amman (capital of Jordan) [4] . . . . (n., f.) عَمّان

Oman [4] . . . . (n., f.) عُمان

at (expresses possession with possessive pronouns) [5] . . . . (adv.) عِندَ

name of the letter *'ayn* [4] . . . . (n., f.) عين

غ

name of the letter *ġayn* [4] . . . . (n., f.) غين

ف

name of the letter *fā'* [3] . . . . (n., f.) فاء

Fez (town in Morocco) [4] . . . . (n., f.) فاس

furṣa saʿīda (literally: *happy opportunity = pleased to meet you*) [1] . . . . فُرْصة سَعيدة.

Palestine [4] . . . . (n., f.) فِلَسطين

in [4] . . . . (prep.) في

ق

name of the letter *qāf* [3] . . . . (n., f.) قاف

Cairo (capital of Egypt) [4] . . . . (n., f.) القاهِرَة

Jerusalem (capital of Palestine) [4] . . . . (n., f.) القُدْس

Qatar [4] . . . . (n., f.) قَطَر

pen, pencil [5] . . . . (n., m.) قَلَم ج أقلام

a little bit; slightly [3] . . . . قَليلاً

ك

name of the letter *kāf* . . . . (n., f.) كاف

book [5] . . . . (n., m.) كِتاب ج كُتُب

chair [6] . . . . (n., m.) كُرسِيّ ج كَراسٍ

Kuwait [4] . . . . (n., f.) الكُوَيت

how [3] . . . . كَيفَ

How are you? [3] . . . . كَيفَ الحال؟

ل

no [2] . . . . (negative particle) لا

not bad [3] . . . . لا بأس

name of the letter *lām* [5] . . . . (n., f.) لام

Lebanon [4] . . . . (n., m.) لُبنان

blackboard [6] . . . . (n. m.) لَوْح ج أَلواح

Libya [4] . . . . (n., f.) ليبيا

م

what's new; what's going on [3] . . . . ما أَخْبارُك

pencil sharpener [6] . . . . (n., f.) مِبراة ج مَبارٍ / مِبْرَيات

madda (a diacritical mark that signifies a *hamza* followed by *alif*) [6] . (n., f.) مَدّة ج مَدّات

city [4] . . . . (n., f.) مَدينة ج مُدُن

hello (greeting) [1] . . . . مَرَحباً

good evening (greeting) [1] . . . . مَساء الخَيْر

good evening (response) [1] . . . . مَساء النور

tape recorder [5] . . . . (n., f.) مُسَجِّلة ج مُسَجِّلات

ruler [6] . . . . (n., f.) مِسْطَرة ج مَساطِر

Muscat (capital of Oman) [4] . . . . (n., f.) مَسْقَط

Egypt [4] . . . . (n., f.) مِصْر

good–bye [1] . . . . مَعَ السَلامَة

Morocco [4] . . . . (n., m.) المَغْرِب

key [5] . . . . (n., m.) مِفْتاح ج مَفاتيح

eraser [6] . . . . (n., f.) مِمْحاة ج مَماحٍ/مِمْحَيات

from, of [4] . . . . (prep.) مِن

proper noun (woman's name) [2] . . . . (n., f.) مَنال

Manama (capital of Bahrain) [4] . . . . (n., f.) المَنامة

Mauritania [4] . . . . (n., f.) موريتانيا

Mogadishu (capital of Somalia) [4] . . . . . . (n., f.) موقاديشو

name of the letter *mīm* [5] . . . . (n., f.) ميم

ن

window [6] . . . . نافِذة ج نَوافِذ (.n., f)

proper noun (man's name) [2] . . . . نِزار (.n., m)

we [5] . . . . نَحْنُ (.pron., pl)

relative adjective [5] . . . . نِسْبَة (.n., f)

eyeglasses [5] . . . . نَظّارة ج نَظّارات (.n., f)

yes [2] . . . . نَعَم(particle)

Nouakchott (capital of Mauritania) [4] . . . . نواكشوط (.n., f)

name of the letter *nūn* [2] . . . . نون (.n., f)

ه

name of the letter *hā'* [5] . . . . هاء (.n., f)

telephone [5] . . . . هاتِف ج هَواتِف (.n., m)

proper noun (woman's name) [2] . . . . هالة (.n., f)

they (m. pl.) [5] . . . . هُمْ (.pron., m., pl)

they (m./f. dual) [5] . . . . هُما (pron., m/f., dual)

they (f. pl.) [5] . . . . هُنَّ (.pron., f., pl)

he [2] . . . . هُوَ (.pron., m)

she [2] . . . . هِيَ (.pron., f)

و

name of the letter *wāw* [1] . . . . واو (.n., f)

sheet of paper [6] . . . . وَرَقة ج وَرَقات (.n., f)

wa 'alaykumu s-salām (response to *as-salāmu 'alaykum*) [1] . . . . وَعَلَيْكُمُ السَلام

homeland [4] . . . . وَطَن ج أوطان (.n., m) state [5] . . . . (n., f.) وِلاية ج وِلايات

Wichita [4] . . . . (n., f.) ويتِشِطا

ي

name of the letter *yā'* [2] . . . . (n., f.) ياء

Utah [4] . . . . (n., f.) يوطا

Yemen [4] . . . . (n., m.) اليَمَن

Illustration Credits